Walking Through the Doorways of Destiny

Walking Through the Doorways of Destiny

A Motivational Guide for Living

Arthur L. Mackey, Jr.

Pneuma Life PUBLISHING

Walking Through the Doorways of Destiny

Printed in the United States of America
Copyright ©1997
Arthur L. Mackey, Jr.

Walking Through the Doorways of Destiny
ISBN 1-56229-420-2

Pneuma Life Publishing
Post Office Box 885
Lanham, MD 20703-0885
301-577-4052
Website - http://www.pneumalife.com

Contents

Dedication
Acknowledgments
Foreword
Preface

Chapter   **Page**

About the Author
Scripture References
Selected Bibliography
Notes

Dedication

I dedicate this book to my wife, my baby, Brenda Jackson Mackey. Thank you for your support and encouragement.

Acknowledgments

Special thanks to Derwin Stewart and the staff of Pneuma Life Publishing who helped to make this dream of destiny a reality.

To Ava Jackson and the late Kathline Brown for typing the original manuscript.

Foreword

In my travels throughout this nation, I am often asked about my opinion concerning the spiritual condition of the church. The usual negative focus in these conversations is geared toward the lack of spiritual growth, the abuse of spiritual authority, and the boredom of the traditionally repetitious, liturgical church.

My response comes from a Scripture that addresses the reason for past problems of the church:

My people are destroyed for lack of knowledge (Hosea 4:6).

What we do not know about God, the Scriptures, holiness, and biblical principles has caused spiritual deficiency in the body of Christ.

Yet now, in these latter days, the church is experiencing a great awakening through the Holy Spirit. The body of Christ must be prepared—with zeal and passion—for every spiritual encounter. We can meet the needs of our searching generation by increasing in knowledge, understanding, information, and practical application of the principles essential for spiritual success.

Prudent application of these principles are easily understood in the inspired writings of Rev. Arthur L. Mackey, Jr. in this and in his previous book, *The Biblical Principles of Success.*

Having known this anointed author and minister of God since 1977, I am overwhelmed with godly pride as I pen this foreword. Arthur, an adolescent at the time, was a holy youth, loving the things of God as he followed in the path laid for him by his reverend father and godly mother, as well as his grandfather.

Learning has always been the thrust that propelled Arthur and the entire Mackey family. His zeal toward God and understanding of the Scriptures, as inspired by the Holy Spirit, will indeed transform and increase your spiritual comprehension as it has mine. God bless and give you understanding.

Elder Donnie McClurkin
Perfecting Church, Detroit, Michigan

Preface

Destiny is the God-given source of motivation, the predetermined plan that compels us to succeed through the storms and the struggles of life even when we were not supposed to make it, according to the dictates and standards of man.

Do you have questions about your personal destiny and how it is linked to something bigger than yourself? Do you ever wonder how God opens new doorways of destiny for your spiritual development and simultaneously closes doors that led to your personal disaster and destruction? What must you do to hit the target and fulfill God's specific purpose for your life?

As you ponder these questions and read these pages, keep a pen and paper within reach. I believe God will shed light on your experiences and provide the answers you seek.

As we approach the twenty-first century, our nation is plagued by issues such as Dr. Jack Kevorkian's assisted suicide, abortion on demand, and poverty—enemies that destroy destiny. We must gain a crystal clear understanding of our destiny, which was designed by God Himself. We need the Holy Spirit as our motivational guide for living as never before.

Walking Through the Doorways of Destiny addresses the developmental stages and the issues that every believer must experience in this journey called life. I pray that it will bless everyone who reads it.

Chapter 1

The Essence of Destiny

"The greatest thing in this world is not so much where we are but in what direction we are moving."—O. W. Holmes

In May 1993, the Mt. Sinai Baptist Church Anniversary Committee held a service in celebration of the initial release of my first book, *The Biblical Principles of Success—A Practical Guide for Living*. Family and friends came out to support this new aspect of my ministry.

Following the festivities, my wife Brenda and I went out for a midnight snack at a local diner. After we were seated at our table and the waiter took our order, Brenda told me, "I have a surprise to tell you."

When the waiter returned with our food, Brenda congratulated me on being an author and then said, "I also congratulate you because you are going to be a father!"

She had just learned from her doctor that she was six weeks pregnant with destiny—a precious gift sent from above. I was totally elated over the thought of a new addition to our family.

A few days later we took the sound advice of family and close friends and visited the office of the best obstetrician on Long Island. He gave Brenda a routine check-up and sent her for a sonogram. To our dismay, he discovered major complications that could threaten the birth of our baby . . . and the sequence of destiny.

Together with the obstetrician, we monitored the matter closely. After we stood on and confessed God's Word together for a few months, Brenda had to be placed on total bed rest. Every single development from this stage in the pregnancy was extremely critical.

Destiny's Timing

In those moments of uncertainty, I learned more clearly what it means to believe God and not see the results instantly.

By faith, Brenda's pregnancy reached the six-and-a-half month point. Everyone thought, from a medical standpoint, that Brenda would deliver prematurely in the seventh month, but that wasn't destiny in this particular case.

My father, the Rev. Dr. Arthur L. Mackey, Sr., pastor of the Mt. Sinai Baptist Church in Roosevelt, was born prematurely, weighing only three pounds and two ounces at birth. His first bed was a small dresser drawer. God brought him through victoriously, and today my father's powerful testimony encourages others in their faith.

During the weeks that followed, family and friends surrounded us with an atmosphere of Christ–centered confessions of faith in the midst of very frustrating circumstances. When Brenda reached the seventh month, I had a peace in my spirit that our baby was going to be carried to full term.

The promise of Philippians 4:7 became a reality in my life:

And the peace of God, which passeth all understanding, shall keep your hearts and minds through Christ Jesus.

Isaiah 26:3 also took on new meaning for me:

Thou wilt keep him in perfect peace, whose mind is stayed on thee: because he trusteth in thee.

As the days and months passed, there was a supernatural sense of expectation that arose in our spirits. We knew in our hearts that destiny would be delivered and fulfilled.

Giving Birth to the Future

The scheduled date of delivery projected by our obstetrician was January 15, 1994–Rev. Dr. Martin Luther King, Jr.'s birthday.

When Brenda and I went for her final checkup with the obstetrician, we discovered to our dismay that new complications were looming over the pregnancy.

The following day, January 14–one day before the due date–Brenda went back to the doctor's office for a stress test, and everything showed up fine.

The Holy Spirit, however, divinely impressed upon my heart to have Brenda go for another sonogram right away. To the doctor's surprise, the sonogram showed that the baby was in danger.

That particular day I was already scheduled to do the opening and closing prayer at the hospital for its annual Rev. Dr. Martin Luther King, Jr. celebration.

Brenda was rushed immediately to the delivery room on the third floor of the hospital. I checked on her and then went back to the first floor of the hospital for the service.

After the highly anointed celebration, which included an inspiring youth choir from Pennsylvania, I returned to the delivery room on the third floor. Brenda, her sister Debbie, a Spirit-filled nurse, and I had a powerful prayer and pulled down some major strongholds of the enemy.

We claimed the truth of this passage:

For though we walk in the flesh, we do not war after the flesh: (For the weapons of our warfare are not carnal, but mighty through God to the pulling down of strong holds;) Casting down imaginations, and every high thing that exalteth itself against the knowledge of God, and bringing into captivity every thought to the obedience of Christ (2 Corinthians 10:3–5).

We also prayed in the Spirit, according to Romans 8:26,27:

Likewise the Spirit also helpeth our infirmities: for we know not what we should pray for as we ought: but the Spirit itself maketh intercession for us with groanings which cannot be uttered. And he that searcheth the hearts knoweth what is the mind of the Spirit, because he maketh intercession for the saints according to the will of God.

After much intercession, agony, pain, and travail, our precious daughter of destiny, Yolanda Alicia Mackey, was born weighing nine pounds and four ounces at 4:45 p.m.

When I held Yolanda in my arms, I was holding the future.

Victory in High Risk Situations

The completion of the birthing process unlocked a doorway of destiny, new opportunities, and memories for our family.

Considering the medical data we had received earlier, it was apparent that Yolanda's full-term birth was a miracle. I was truly humbled by seeing God intervene in the situation because I know many people who have lost their babies by miscarriages, stillbirths, and crib deaths.

The doctors did their job well with precision and perfect timing, and I salute them for their marvelous work. But it was Dr. Jesus, the Master of Destiny, Who guided them and decided to save the seed for His purpose and glory.

Our obstetrician, in his highly respected medical opinion, doubted that Brenda would carry full term because he considered her pregnancy to be high risk.

Many people who are reading this chapter right now are in high risk situations and compromising predicaments. God can bring you through victoriously, as 1 Corinthians 15:57 states:

> But thanks be to God, which giveth us the victory through our Lord Jesus Christ.

Spiritually Pregnant

Experience has taught me that God, our Creator, desires that we all get spiritually pregnant. By this analogy, I mean that we must have a full, fertile, and enriching vision of victory developing in our spiritual uterus while we wait on the Lord in worship and praise.

This truth is confirmed by Isaiah 66:7–9, which states:

> Before she travailed, she brought forth; before her pain came, she was delivered of a man child. Who hath heard such a thing? who hath seen such things? Shall the earth be made to bring forth in one day? or shall a nation be born at once? for as soon as Zion travailed, she brought forth her children. Shall I bring to the birth, and not cause to bring forth? saith the Lord: shall I cause to bring forth, and shut the womb? saith thy God.

Although these prophetic verses specifically refer to Israel becoming a nation, this prophecy also holds an initial key component leading to the imminent return of Jesus Christ as foreshadowed and foretold in Isaiah 66:15–17 and 2 Thessalonians 1:7–9.

The fulfillment of the Isaiah 66:7–9 prophecy occurred in May 1948, when Israel was officially declared a national state, including parts of Palestine. This prophecy also foreshadowed the birth of the church, a new nation under the leadership and Lordship of Jesus Christ.

The Word of God confirms this statement:

But ye are a chosen generation, a royal priesthood, an holy nation, a peculiar people; that ye should shew forth the praises of him who hath called you out of darkness into his marvelous light (1 Peter 2:9).

We must get lined up in the spiritual birth canal of Christ's purposes and give birth to divine destiny in our personal lives. That is how we become the "chosen generation."

Why Were You Born?

Not everyone will have children in the physical sense, but everyone can give birth to destiny and purpose in his or her own life and provide essential support to people who are truly hurting.

Romans 12:15 affirms this truth:

Rejoice with them that do rejoice, and weep with them that weep.

Why was the apostle Paul saved, single, and satisfied? Because God called him to be a spiritual father to countless hundreds of thousands of believers who would hear his sermons and read his writings for generations to come.

Paul explained the reason for his contentment:

Blessed be the God and Father our Lord Jesus Christ, who hath blessed us with all spiritual blessings in heavenly places in Christ: According as he hath chosen us in him before the foundation the world, that we should be holy and without blame before him in love: Having predestinated us unto the adoption of children by Jesus Christ to himself, according to the good pleasure of his will (Ephesians 1:3–5).

God the Father has blessed us with all kinds of spiritual gifts and chose us even before He formed the earth.

Before the Creator said, "Let there be light," He had already established a plan to adopt us into the family of God through Christ Jesus—even before we were born.

Walking Through the Doorways of Destiny teaches us that God was totally aware of our birth. El Shaddai, the God Who is more than enough, the all-sufficient One, knows the very moment, the actual second, that we were born.

Once we discover the real reason why we were born and begin to walk through the doorway of our personal destiny, we will be instantly listed on satan's most-wanted list. We will have demonic hit-men on our trail, but Jesus has already put them under our feet.

In order for divine destiny to be realized, we must breathe deeply and push hard like a mother who is completely dilated and in full labor. Our destiny, like that newborn, will soon emerge. Sometimes we will groan in the spirit, but if we keep on breathing and pushing, we will give birth to the future.

Headed in the Right Direction

When my mother, Dr. Frances W. Mackey, was pregnant with me, her doctor discovered in the early stages of the pregnancy that I was stuck in her fallopian tube. The doctors and his staff performed major surgery on my mother and strategically moved me from my mother's fallopian tube, positioning me correctly in her uterus. This procedure made it possible for me to pass through the birth canal during labor and delivery.

Sometimes Jesus Christ, the Divine Director of Personal Development and Optimum Level of Success, has to strategically reposition us correctly in the spiritual birth canal in order for destiny to be accomplished. Jesus Christ is the Master Motivator of a massive movement of divine destiny based on a deep abiding faith in God.

Jesus Christ understands the triumphs and the tragedies of our todays. He foresees the trials and tribulations that we will encounter tomorrow. As we get closer to Jesus Christ, we get closer to destiny.

By the actualization of our purpose and the realization of our unfolding, divinely appointed destiny should create an innate sense of knowing what to do—not by our own might and power but through the Spirit of the Lord.

Jesus said:

> To this end was I born, and for this cause came I into the world, that I should bear witness unto the truth. Every one that is of the truth heareth my voice (John 18:37).

When we search and discover the truth concerning our identity—who we really are in Christ, and why we are here—and when we walk in the divine revelation of that knowledge, we are then walking toward the doorways of destiny.

Jesus Christ is the Master Motivator of a massive movement of divine destiny based on a deep abiding faith in God.

Chapter 2

What is Destiny?

"A consistent man believes in destiny; a capricious man in chance."
— Benjamin Disraeli

Destiny is a fascinating, intriguing, and thought-provoking subject that is of tremendous importance to the very existence, foundation, and future of the church in modern society. Both the Old and New Testaments use the terms chosen, ordained, and predestined to describe divine destiny.

In order to clearly comprehend the true essence of destiny that is developed in earthen vessels, we must first answer several questions:

Is destiny the same as purpose? No. Destiny and purpose may be interrelated scriptural themes, but they are not synonymous.

Is destiny a theological concept that is too deep for a lay person to understand? No.

What is destiny?

Destiny is not a current buzz word or new cliche designed to move the masses though media ministry. Destiny is not a passing teaching trend that fails to provide depth and substance in uncertain times.

Destiny is a predetermined plan sent straight from the very mind of God, the Creator of all life, concerning the fate and future of His prized creation, humanity. Destiny is a preordained prophecy that must be executed no matter what. Destiny is a plan about which God won't change His mind.

Destiny is quite different in nature from purpose because destiny can be road blocked only temporarily. Even if God has to raise up and use somebody else in a completely different generation, destiny must be fulfilled. And God will use any means He deems necessary to accomplish His predestined plans, purpose, and directives in the earth.

If God has to use a stone to proclaim the word of faith concerning destiny, it will be preached one way or another. (See Luke 19:40.) The bottom line is the destiny–determining factor that truly dictates our fate and future.

In a more natural sense, destiny is the inevitable consequences of our daily decisions, actions, and affairs of life–the overall quality of our spiritual, social, political, and economic existence.

The Real McCoy

Elijah J. McCoy, a mechanical engineer of African-American descent who lived during the mid-to-late 1800s until the early 1900s, strove for excellence. An ingenious inventor, McCoy created the state-of-the-art instrument that made it possible to lubricate specific parts of machinery while they were still in motion.

Every major company that handles mass production machinery—such as that used in manufacturing automobiles, motorcycles, trains, planes, rockets, boats, and cruise-liners–utilizes McCoy's technology. This lubricating cup revolutionized the entire industry, cut labor costs, reduced manufacturing time, and enhanced the profit margin significantly.

Although McCoy's heritage, race, and ancestry had closed many doors for him, God opened a divine doorway of destiny—a door no one could close. Even today, when mechanical engineers and technological experts speak about top-notch, quality work, they call it "the real McCoy."

Through the three D's of divine direction, godly decisions, and determination—and by tapping into the inner reservoir of God-given resources—you too can overcome the stigmas of society and leave a lasting impact upon history.

Destiny's Three D's

Destiny becomes real by practicing the three D's. Let's see how these can work for you in your life:

1. When the arrow of your inner compass points in the same direction as Jesus, you are headed toward the doorways of destiny.

2. When the zig-zag lines on the monitor of your personal decisions match the providential pattern of Jehovah-Jireh, the Lord God our Provider, you are headed toward the doorways of destiny.

3. When you are determined to catch the vision of victory and never give up on feeding the hungry and homeless, clothing the naked, and rescuing the perishing, you are getting closer to the doorways of destiny.

Destiny is predetermined by decisions that are made both by the Creator and His creation—by God and by mankind. If you receive Jesus Christ as your personal Lord and Savior, Healer, and Deliverer, you will have changed your destiny in the here and now—as well as in the by and by.

God's preordained plan for our lives is the course that we are called upon to take and ultimately expected to complete—yet not forced to finish. If we don't finish the course, God will raise up someone else to fulfill the race toward destiny, but we will surely suffer the consequences for our decision to ignore His will.

We don't have to be swift to be in this race; we just have to finish our God-given course of destiny. We must endure to the end.

Between Two Destinies

The Bible presents a balanced message concerning destiny. First of all, God desires that no one should perish. The Bible also clearly states that many people will be eternally damned because of their unrighteous deeds.

The apostle Peter made this precise point:

> The Lord is not slack concerning his promise, as some men count slackness; but is longsuffering to us-ward, not willing that any should perish, but that all should come to repentance. But the day of the Lord will come as a thief in the night; in the which the heavens shall pass away with a great noise, and the elements shall melt with fervent heat, the earth also and works that are therein shall be burned up (2 Peter 3:9,10).

We have the choice between two destinies: heaven or hell, blessings or curses, life or death, faith or fear, Jesus or satan. The choice is ours.

Deuteronomy 30:19 confirms this statement of faith:

> I call heaven and earth to record this day against you, that I have set before you life and death, blessing and cursing: therefore choose life, that both thou and thy seed may live.

God has preordained, preplanned, and predetermined directives that will occur no matter what. The Creator chose us for His perfect plan, ". . . before the foundation of the world, that we should be holy and without blame before him in love" (Ephesians 1:4).

The Time Factor

God is not pressured for time. God created the concept of time, but He is not controlled by it. The Creator of the universe has plenty of time:

> But, beloved, be not ignorant of this one thing, that one day is with the Lord as a thousand years, and a thousand years as one day (2 Peter 3:8).

Such is not the case with humanity. Mankind without God equals failure, and our days are numbered. Mankind's time is running out, day by day like sand in an hour glass. Each day takes us one day closer to death and the judgment.

> Man that is born of a woman is of few days, and full of trouble. . . . Seeing his days are determined, the number of his months are with thee, thou has appointed his bounds that he cannot pass (Job 14:1,5).

In other words, God has all the time He wants and needs, and we have only an allotted period of time, a limited boundary that He chooses to give us. We can believe for extra time by faith, but when it is all over, then comes the judgment.

Hebrew 9:27 attests to this scriptural fact:

> And as it is appointed unto men once to die, but after this the judgment.

It most certainly behooves each and every one of us to get in touch with the essence of destiny. We don't need to miss the time of our visitation (Luke 19:42–44) because of a lack of knowledge that could ruin a potential move of God in our lives.

Now is the time to grasp the Master's motivating message and meet Him personally at the doorway of destiny.

Just in Time

A few years ago, after I had graduated from college in Virginia, I was driving to work when suddenly the lights on the control panel of my car started flashing rapidly. The speedometer quickly dropped from 45 m.p.h. to 30 to 15 to 5. I couldn't imagine what was wrong since the car had just been in the shop for a tune-up.

As the lights continued to flash, I pulled the car over to the side of the road. When I popped open the hood, flames raged uncontrollably. I instantly jumped out of the car and ran quickly in the opposite direction just as my car exploded! Watching my vehicle burn from only 25 feet away, I realized how close I had come to being killed. In that moment, my entire life passed before me.

Still in shock, I stood on the side of the highway while car and truck drivers passed by, staring at the devastation. When the police and fire department finally arrived, they put out the raging flames, and a tow truck pulled away the remains.

I knew it was a miracle that I made it out of the burning car in time.

That was only one of several near-death experiences I have had. In addition, my life has been a series of tests, trials, and tribulations that were designed by the devil to destroy my destiny.

I know from experience that it is only by the grace of God that we live, move, and have our being. Our very breath is a definite sign that God still has work for us to do. Our challenge is to help someone else who is having a difficult time breathing spiritually as well as physically.

When I was in elementary school, I had a terrible case of asthma that prevented me from breathing properly. The persistent wheezing racked my body. At one point, I could not even go to school because of my severe sickness.

Since my asthmatic condition kept me at home constantly, sick and gasping for breath, I was held back in school and did not advance that year to the next grade with my classmates.

Many years later, during junior high school and after much asthmatic medicine, I received the baptism in the Holy Spirit with the evidence of speaking in tongues. When that happened, I was simultaneously healed of asthma.

That didn't change the fact, however, that all the way through junior high school, I was still one grade behind.

At the end of tenth grade, however, I took a special three-month course and doubled up on my subjects, skipped the eleventh grade, went to the twelfth grade, and graduated with my right class.

Destiny was certainly delayed but not destroyed.

God knows how to breathe into our present predicaments and restore our broken, bruised, and battered lives.

Never Alone

I am reminded of a little girl whose father was recently murdered in cold blood by an insane lunatic. Although the killer is behind bars today, that does not ease the pain this young girl feels or the fact that she still misses her dad. Every day she waits for him to walk through the front door, but he never comes because he is gone for good.

As she stares at the door, she vividly remembers the precious songs that he sang to her and the bedtime stories he read to her each night. Yet as she looks at the door, she realizes that never again—at least not on this side of Zion—will she hear his footsteps.

He won't be there to see his daughter walk down the aisle to receive her diploma on graduation day. As she begins to step through her doorway of educational destiny, her sole motivation will be the ever-present memory of her father's tired face as he came through the front door after a hard day at work. He worked those long, hard hours to pay for his daughter's education and, in essence, paved the way for her future.

The essence of destiny does not mean that since God has plans for our lives, we will not experience hard times. Destiny is discovered when we learn to appreciate the nature of the words spoken by Jesus Christ nearly 2,000 years ago. In the Great Commission the Master said:

Lo, I am with you alway, even unto the end of the world. Amen (Matthew 28:20).

Jesus Christ did not say that everything would be a bed of roses, always smelling nice and pleasant. Jesus Christ did not say we would never feel like turning back to our own personal Egypts. Jesus Christ never said that we would not experience moments of crisis on our journey through the jungles of life.

Our God promised, in no uncertain terms:

I will never leave thee, nor forsake thee (Hebrews 13:5).

God has paved a road to progress even through the jungles of life.

When your back is up against the wall of worry and doubt, God is there. Stop doubting and start trusting in Him. When you feel like giving up on your dreams, goals, hopes, and aspirations, hold on. God is right there.

Lives Snuffed Out

With sadness in his voice, the radio newsman reported: "Susan Smith, the twenty-three-year-old Union, South Carolina mother has confessed that she murdered her two sons, Michael, age three, and Alex, 14 months."

I heard this tragic news that shocked the nation as I was on my way to pick up my twin nephews, Jonathan and Joshua, and my niece, Amanda, for school.

As I walked upstairs to my sister Frances' room where she was combing the kids' hair, she said, "Arthur, did you hear that Susan Smith actually killed her own two children?"

All that day at work, in the supermarket, on the radio, television, and even in the church, everyone was asking, "How could she murder her own children? Those beautiful kids! How could she do it?"

Had she given up on life? Did she have some selfish motive in ridding herself of the boys? What caused her to block out everything she had ever been taught, deny her conscience, and murder her own children?

About nine days before Smith's shocking confession, this murderer told the world via television that a gun-toting, car-jacking black man had taken her two precious little boys. The general public bought her erroneous story. That says something about the state of our nation when we tend to believe and embrace stereotypes so quickly.

When Susan Smith failed portions of a lie detector test, police detectives and their investigative units began to question her story.

I pray for the people of Union, South Carolina, and the people of the United States that this situation will serve as a lesson to end racial stereotypes in the hearts and minds of the masses.

I also pray that the world will realize that when Susan Smith allowed her two sons to roll down that ramp at John D. Long Lake while strapped in theirs belts and locked in their car seats, that Michael and Alex won't be able to fulfill their personal destiny. God will have to put His permissive will, His back-up plan, into action. Someone else will have to finish the earthly work that those boys were designed to accomplish.

We will never know—at least on this side of Zion—what great things Michael and Alex would have accomplished in their lifetimes. Like babies who are aborted, their lives were snuffed out before they had a chance to fulfill their destinies.

All is not lost, however, because every bloodwashed believer in Jesus Christ will most certainly see our young brothers in Christ, Michael and Alex, in heaven. Because of their innocence, their eternal destiny is now far greater than their earthy destiny.

I also pray for Susan Smith to realize the tragic fact that she has toyed with God's most precious creation, children, and that she might truly get her heart right with God Himself.

Jesus Christ spoke about the eternal consequences of damaging a child:

> At the same time came the disciples unto Jesus, saying, Who is the greatest in the kingdom of heaven? And Jesus called a little child unto him, and set him in the midst of them, And said, Verily I say unto you, Except ye be converted, and become as little children, ye shall not enter into the kingdom of heaven.

> Whosoever therefore shall humble himself as this little child, the same is greatest in the kingdom of heaven. And whoso shall receive one such little child in my name receiveth me. But whoso shall offend one of these little ones which believe in me, it were better for him that a millstone were hanged about his neck, and that he were drowned in the depth of the sea (Matthew 18:1–6).

For anyone who is playing with the future of a child, it behooves us all to repent and truly get right with God.

How is Your Self-Esteem?

We need to get out of the front seat and let God take control. Abortion is so tragic because it instantly terminates purpose and severely delays destiny for countless generations. Suicide is a one-way ticket to hell because you can't ask for forgiveness once you are dead.

Don't give up because the struggles of life will always rage like the stormy sea. We must have faith because without it we cannot please God or find the essence of destiny.

Faith is also necessary to build our self-esteem.

I am not talking about the selfish philosophy of me, myself, and I. Christian self-esteem is not a matter of discovering who you are. It is a matter of finding who you are in Christ.

Self-esteem is an important aspect of this discussion concerning destiny. Our inner picture of ourselves shapes our destiny probably more than anything else.

Jesus told us to love our neighbors "as ourselves." The prerequisite to loving those around us is to learn to love ourselves first. I call this lesson from the Master "Self-Esteem 101."

Everyone has a role to play. No one is insignificant to the Creator. We need to develop a Christian-based self-esteem and a balanced, Christ-centered, can-do attitude. Then we can begin to alleviate the pain and demolish the prison cells of bondage that hold us captive and keep us from God's perfect will.

Through Christ, we are predestined to arise from devastation, and we are destined to be overcomers, more than conquerors, and even more than successful.

Stop sabotaging your self-esteem and resolve right now to base your daily actions and attitudes on the precise, unimpeachable, and unadulterated gospel of Jesus Christ. Decide today to walk through your personal doorway of destiny.

**Destiny is a plan about which
God won't change His mind.**

Chapter 3

The Divine Door Opener

"The only limit to our realization of tomorrow will be our doubts of today."–Franklin D. Roosevelt

On the day that Colin Ferguson decided to take a loaded rifle and aim it indiscriminately at commuters on a Long Island train, he became a tool in satan's hand. As people begged for their lives, he shot them point blank, killing a mother on her way home from work, a father sitting beside his son, and several others, including the brother-in-law of one of my co-workers.

My father, the Rev. Arthur L. Mackey, Sr., arrived at the scene and witnessed what he later described as a total blood bath. Although he had seen many terrible tragedies in his days as a pastor, this was the worst. Still, in the midst of satan's carnage, my father was able to pray with many of the victims.

Satan and his demonic cohorts are thieves that rob innocent victims of their divine destiny by stealing, killing, and destroying their hopes, dreams, aspirations, and their very lives.

The skin color of the crime suspect does not matter. If the crime involves stealing, killing, or destroying innocent victims, it is satanically influenced. The devil's job is to steal, kill, and destroy life.

Before a death wish comes from the lips of the mob boss, it is inspired by satan. Before a drive-by shooting occurs, it is planned by satan. In other words, there are two major forms of destiny—God's preordained plan for your life and satan's scheme to ruin your very existence.

> The thief cometh not, but for to steal, and to kill, and to destroy: I am come that they might have life, and that they might have it more abundantly (John 10:10).

Demon spirits lurk at the root of every devastating, violent crime—whether it is the bombing of the New York World Trade Center or the Oklahoma City Federal Building; the brutal murder of Nicole Simpson and Ronald Goldman; the Long Island Railroad gunman massacre; or a rape or murder in your own community.

The forces of pure evil constantly seek to steal, kill, and destroy you before you can walk through your personal doorways of destiny.

Where Was God?

Within a few seconds, the bombing of the Alfred Murray Federal Building brutally wounded federal employees and many of their precious children on the second floor day-care center. Others were instantly blown to pieces or crushed by falling concrete as the bomb exploded.

I will never forget the tragic image of a fireman carrying a burned child who later died. The paramedics, nurses, and doctors could not even determine the sex of the child at first because the baby was burned so badly. Of the 168 people confirmed dead from the cowardly blast, 19 of them were children.

Satan knows his job, and he will carry it out with a vengeance through anyone who opens his or her heart and mind to the spirit of hatred and violence.

After the bombing many people asked, "Where was God when this tragedy occurred in Oklahoma City?"

God was there. He was in the firemen and rescue workers who immediately came from across the country to provide aid and comfort to the disaster victims.

God was in the governor and the people of Oklahoma who scheduled an inter-faith prayer memorial when other states would have rioted in uncontrolled rage.

God was also in the words of wisdom proclaimed by priests, rabbis, and distinguished spiritual leaders.

Most of all, God was and is in the hearts and minds of countless numbers of genuinely concerned people who still believe that good will finally overcome evil and God's truth will prevail over the devil's mind games of deception.

The Door of Your Mind

The apostle Paul stated in 1 Corinthians 16:9 that when God opened a great and effectual door in his ministry, there were "many adversaries"—the enemies of divine destiny—who blocked the door. They cannot close a God-opened door, but they will surely try to block it.

When God opens doors in your life, you are not the only one who walks through them. Satan also walks through in an effort to stop you. The devil can't close the door that God has opened, but he will certainly do his best to stop you from fulfilling your destiny.

In order to fulfill your divine destiny, you must be acutely aware of the enemies of destiny and know how to defeat them in Jesus' name.

Your mind is a doorway of destiny that God opened up and will not close. Why? Because He created humankind as free-will agents who can make choices. Our decisions, however, affect not only ourselves but others as well.

Satan wants to walk through the door of your mind and make you an enemy of destiny.

Colin Ferguson and the Oklahoma bombers became instruments of satan to prevent the fulfillment of personal destiny for many people. These senseless, hateful exploits occurred because men opened their minds to satan and were used by him.

At the same time that satan prowls around, God seeks radical Christian warriors who desire to save lives—not destroy them. If we open our hearts and minds and get to know God intimately, we will be strong and do exploits that will bring healing, deliverance, salvation, and peace to our hurting world.

Fascinated With O. J.

God knows more about you and your personal DNA and genetic make-up than the experts in the high-profile O. J. Simpson trial. God wants you to be as consumed with His Word as some people were with the daily courtroom proceedings and the continuous trial updates.

Why did this trial become such an integral part of our culture? People were engrossed with the "trial of the century" because it symbolized in real-life drama all the enemies of destiny—children robbed of their mother, the brutal killing of a young man, and grieving families devastated by the loss of their murdered loved ones.

Why were Americans so fascinated by this tragic display of man's inhumanity to man? Because as a nation, we ourselves are abused and bleeding from satan's deadly wounds.

We need to walk through God's doorways of destiny and discover His divine developmental stages of life step by step. Then we will be on the pathway to true and lasting inner healing.

As the days, years, and decades pass, I pray that we will realize that the Door, Jesus Christ, is the only Way. Only He can open the many doorways of destiny in our lives that no man can close.

When God Intervenes

When my mother was told she had a tumor, the doctor insisted she needed major surgery. My mother and our entire family began to pray fervently for her healing for several months.

After much intercessory prayer in the midnight hours, the morning of the operation finally arrived. My father, my sisters, my wife Brenda, and I were all together early that morning at the hospital. When my mother came out already prepared for surgery, we decided to have one more word of prayer with her.

In the operating room, the doctors began to work on my mother, not realizing that God had already miraculously intervened. To their astonishment, they could not find the tumor because God had totally healed my mother.

God opened the door of healing for her, and she believed in it and walked through it. Of course, all healing does not happen instantaneously.

My mother also had serious back problems for several years. At one point she could hardly walk. In fact, she had to learn how to walk all over again, and she had to learn to take one step at a time. Every day we put a heating pad on her back and helped her take a few steps.

If she was in too much pain and agony to move, my mother would ring a little bell, and I would come running to see what she needed. The pressure and the pain, however, did not stop her from praising God for the door of healing that He opened through Jesus Christ's life, death, and resurrection. She came through that difficult time by standing on the Word of God in the midst of the pain.

Today she is an extremely busy, dedicated pastor's wife and a former president of the Eastern Baptist Association of Ministers and Ministers' Wives group. When she shares God's Word with audiences, they sit on the edges of their seats to hear a fresh *rhema* word from the Lord.

Step By Step

God does heal our diseases, but God also requires us to rise up in faith so that we can walk step by step through the rough times in any area of life. In other words, you cannot get through every open door overnight.

Sometimes the walk of faith leading to your personal doorway of destiny is relatively short in distance and brings with it quick deliverance. At other times, that faith journey is long, tedious, and hard and includes tremendous struggles as we walk by faith and not by sight. Walking by faith requires total dependence on that which is unseen. This is not easy, but it is mandatory by God.

Our contacts, clout, and cunning won't even crack open the heavily padlocked doors that block our way. If, however, we walk step by step in obedience to God's Word, nothing can stop the bloodwashed believer from receiving the blessing that the Creator wants to bestow on His child.

Although the actual steps of a righteous individual are ordered by the Lord, the journey still has to be personally carried out by each man, woman, boy, or girl. God won't walk through your personal doorway of destiny for you—and neither will your father, mother, step-mother, step-father, sister, brother, aunt, uncle, cousin, niece, nephew, husband, wife, boyfriend, or girlfriend.

Walking through your own personal doorway of destiny that Jesus Christ, the Divine Door Opener, has placed before you is designed to enhance and enrich *your* spiritual development in Christ. Walking through the doorway of destiny is a personal experience.

No one can walk through your doorway of destiny. You have to walk through this door for yourself. You have to seek your own soul's salvation with fear and trembling before the Most High God.

Jesus makes this promise to us:

I know thy works: behold, I have set before thee an open door, and no man can shut it: for thou hast a little strength, and hast kept my word, and hast not denied my name (Revelation 3:8).

When I read this verse, I personalize it. "I know your works, Arthur. Behold, I have set before you, Arthur, an open door, and no man can shut it: for you, Arthur, have a little strength, and have kept My word, and have not denied My name."

God will open doors in our lives that no man can close if we learn to do these four things:

1. Realize our need to depend on the strength of God.

2. Hide His Word in our hearts that we might not sin against Him.

3. Constantly confess the Word of God.

4. Do not deny His holy name.

Nobody can walk through the doorways of destiny with his or her own strength and ability. Neither might, power, nor socio-economic influence opens this door. Our big egos won't even fit through this door.

A Witness for the Lord

I have a close friend who is physically challenged and unable to walk without the assistance of crutches. As a born-again Christian who believes in the baptism of the Holy Ghost and divine healing, he recently became extremely depressed about his condition and began to turn away from God.

God used an annual youth retreat to work on my friend's heart and burdened him to be a more effective witness for the Lord. God opened the door of understanding for my friend to realize that God is still on his side whether his healing manifests in this lifetime or when he walks through that door in heaven and sees Jesus face to face.

With this fresh revelation, my friend is now on fire for Jesus Christ and takes advantage of every single opportunity that God gives him to be a witness for the Lord.

God uses ordinary people to open doors in the lives of others who are hurting.

Every time volunteers from a shelter feed the hungry and the homeless, that is a classic example of God opening doors. Every time prayer partners give gifts to children of single parents at Christmas time or send care packages to college students and members of the armed forces, that is an example of God opening doors through ordinary people who are willing to be a witness for the Lord.

His Eye is On the Sparrow

Jesus Christ, the Master of divine destiny, is concerned about you personally. He wants you to reach your fullest potential on this side of Zion.

God is also concerned about our personal predicaments. How do we know that? Because Jesus said:

Are not two sparrows sold for a farthing? and one of them shall not fall on the ground without your Father. But the very hairs of your head are all numbered. Fear ye not therefore, ye are of more value than many sparrows (Matthew 10:29-31).

If God is concerned about sparrows, just imagine how much He cares about your personal destiny. God has already numbered every hair on your head. Whether you wear a weave, a jheri curl, a crew cut, or an afro—or if you have a bald head—God cares about you personally.

That is why Mrs. C. D. Martin penned these anointed words:

Why should I feel discouraged?
Why should the shadows come?
Why should my heart be lonely and long for heaven and home?
When Jesus is my portion, my constant Friend is He:
His eye is on the sparrow, and I know He watches me.[1]

You can be sure that God is watching over you, protecting and guiding you by His Holy Spirit to help you fulfill His destiny for your life.

Delayed But Not Denied

I remember times in my life when I hit rock-bottom and had no money in my pocket, no food in the refrigerator, and only one set of clothing to wear. My shoes were so worn that they had huge holes in them.

One day, in order to put gas in the car, I counted out 500 pennies and went to the gas station to get five dollars of gas. Yet, I can testify that if you stay faithful to God while you're on the rough and rocky roads of life, He will open doors for you.

In my book, *The Biblical Principles of Success,* I share the true story of the construction of the Roosevelt Public Library. The community had been pushing for this project for well over two decades. Once the long-awaited construction finally began, the architect died, the treasurer died, the brick mason died, and the general contractor went belly up.

Destiny was delayed but not denied, for we still had a vision of victory deep down in our souls. God worked a miracle and completed the construction of that facility through several hard-working and dedicated individuals.

As a young boy in first grade, I had received a flyer showing a picture of the new library that was coming to our community. Throughout my years in elementary school, junior high, senior high, and college, however, the library never materialized.

Years later, God ordered my steps, and with the support of the local churches and the community, I won a five-year seat on the Library Board in 1989.

I'll never forget the feeling of elation I had as I signed the check for the temporary certificate of occupancy for the library at the Hempstead Town Hall Building. That moment, however, was insignificant compared to the day the doors of the Roosevelt Public Library officially opened to the community.

It took a lot of hard work and diligence from the board, the library director, the attorney, the new architect, our staff, and the community to keep working on an impossible situation . . . but we serve a God Who can make the impossible possible.

I was thrilled to walk through the doors of the new library and see all the tables and chairs and bookshelves that had been purchased. The picture of the library that had been only a dream for so many years ago had finally become a reality.

As one senior resident of the community toured the new facility, she cried with tears of joy and said to the library director, "I have waited for 33 years to see this moment."

Thank God destiny was delayed but not denied.

No Slammed Doors

On June 11, 1963, Alabama's Governor George C. Wallace attempted to personally prevent the racial integration of the University of Alabama. By boldly standing right inside the doorway of the school and denying the court-ordered entrance of African-American students who were escorted by representatives from the U.S. Justice Department, he was blocking a divine doorway of destiny that God had determined to open.

God moved upon President John F. Kennedy to approve the federalization of the Alabama National Guard, and Governor Wallace had to move out of the way and allow the African-American students to walk through their educational doorway of destiny. Governor Wallace, who was shot and paralyzed years later, became one of the greatest allies of the underclass and less fortunate in society.

These students and their families had hoped, prayed, and worked so that they might have a better future. They broke ground that paved the way for many other African-American students to pursue higher education.

If you stand on God's Word long enough, God will open doors for you that nobody can close.

Many people think that because they know something negative about you, they can personally slam the door on your future. In essence they say, "I will make sure you don't get ahead." When that happens, remember: If God is for you, He is more than the whole world against you.

Some people may think that if you are down in the dumps, then you are out of the running. But I have news for you: God is not through with you yet. No matter what anyone says, you are not out until God calls you out!

Your future is a matter of divine destiny and not based on the decisions of other people. God has already made His decision, and your calling in life is to say, "yes" to His will. That is not only the key to daily survival but also to daily success.

God won't walk through your personal doorway of destiny for you.

Chapter 4

The Boxer, the Baby, and the Believer

"Unless you try to do something beyond what you have already mastered, you will never grow."–Ralph Waldo Emerson

On Saturday, November 5, 1994, the Rev. George Foreman, a strong 45-year-old, 250-pound black man of destiny, stepped into the boxing ring at the MGM Grand Garden in Las Vegas to regain the title of Heavyweight Boxing Champion of the World.

Most ardent boxing fans will remember that Rev. Foreman lost the title on October 30, 1974, when Mohammed Ali, better known as "The Greatest," knocked Foreman out in the eighth round in Zaire, Africa.

Success, however, is getting up one more time.

In 1987, Rev. Foreman, who also appears in popular television commercials, decided to come out of a ten-year retirement. Why? It was a matter of destiny.

Many television, radio, and newspaper sports analysts, as well as late-night comedians, had their share of criticism and jokes about old Reverend George. Still, he remained undaunted and even more determined to reach his goal.

In fact, the most respected sports anchors and columnists expected Rev. George Foreman to lose the fight to the more youthful, 26-year-old favorite, Michael Moorer. They failed to take into account, however, that the fight was a matter of personal destiny to Rev. George Foreman.

When Rev. Foreman walked into the ring, he was wearing the exact same—but now faded—red trunks he had worn the night Mohammed Ali knocked him out in Zaire 20 years before. After the starting bell rang, Foreman plugged away with each punch, barely making it to the tenth round.

As Rev. Foreman persevered his way to the tenth round, he knew everyone was betting against him. At that point, Rev. Foreman was losing the fight in every sense of the word. Then the miracle of destiny, which is only realized through precise planning, rose up from deep down within his soul.

Rev. George Foreman's right hand landed a powerful punch on Michael Moorer's chin, and the champion fell to the ground. Michael Moorer tried to get back up, but to no avail; he fell right back to the canvas.

As soon as the referee counted Moorer out, Rev. Foreman fell to his knees and offered a prayer of praise and worship to the Master of his destiny. Then he raised his arms proudly in victory.

After the fight, Rev. Foreman stated, "I usually keep the ministry out of the ring, but I wanted this so badly and I was so thankful that I just had to get down on my knees and say, 'Thank You, Jesus!'"

If Rev. Foreman never wins another fight in his life, he has already made history by becoming the oldest heavyweight champion in the world. His victory that night in Las Vegas is a testimony that you can make your vision to fulfill your personal destiny a reality.

Four Doorways to Destiny

You may be asking, "How can I change my present predicament and fulfill my destiny as arranged by the Creator?"

I have found four divinely anointed doorways of destiny that will always lead to lasting success in the midst of, and even through, the storms and struggles of life. These four doorways of destiny are not quick fixes or overnight success strategies.

These four doorways of destiny—and many other divine opportunities—were personally designed by the Door, the Way, the Truth, and the Life Himself—Jesus Christ—with God the Father and the Holy Spirit.

The four doorways of destiny, known as the "four Ps"—prayer, planning, patience, and persistence—are designed to assist us in overcoming any satanic roadblocks that would hinder us from reaching our fullest potential.

The Door of Prayer

Prayer is a dialogue between you and God, in which both of you speak. Prayer is not a monologue where you do all the talking and never listen to the voice of the Holy Spirit.

Communication is the cornerstone of all healthy relationships, and prayer is communication with the Creator of all life. Prayer ties you to the ultimate power source. The Bible says:

Men ought always to pray, and not to faint (Luke 18:1).

Prayer is the foundation of lasting success and godly accomplishments. Prayer teaches you to face your problems by acknowledging them to God, Who can turn your situation around for good.:

And all things, whatsoever ye shall ask in prayer, believing, ye shall receive (Matthew 21:22).

This verse only applies, however, to those things that God's Word promises.

If you are believing for the miracle of never experiencing any hard times, you are surely in for a rude awakening. Yet, if you stand on the promises of God as revealed in the Scriptures, you will find the strength to face the challenges of life and overcome them one by one in Jesus' name.

The Door of Planning

Planning is the God-given ability to organize our short-term and long-term goals and agendas. Without proper planning and goals, we will never know where we want to go. The Bible says:

> Where there is no vision, the people perish: but he that keepeth the law, happy is he (Proverbs 29:18).

Although we know that our destiny is predetermined by God, it is still up to us to plan to fulfill it. The fulfillment of our destiny does not happen by osmosis or because you have a high, moderate, or low I.Q. Destiny begins when you sit down and chart a course on paper concerning how to accomplish your goal. Destiny is fulfilled when you effectively execute the plan until you reach the desired destination.

Poor planning always produces failure and is the eternal enemy of godly success and destiny.

The Door of Patience

Patience is the decision to wait for the seed that you planted to grow into a full-fledged plant. Patience means that you choose to wait on the fulfillment of a promise.

Patience is the ultimate form of confidence. Why? Because you know that God is able to do just what He said.

Patience builds character because it teaches us to occupy our time wisely while waiting for the seed of greatness within us to become a full-grown plant in due season.

The Door of Persistence

Persistence is the assurance of patience. Persistence waters the seeds of greatness within us daily in order to make sure that the promise of patience is fulfilled.

Persistence is a God-given sense of determination that declares destiny will not be denied. Persistence provides balance where people would dare take advantage of patience.

These four doorways of destiny have a far greater impact than I.Q. because anyone can use them and find true success, not overnight, but through the storms and struggles of life.

Ready for the Battle

After winning the fight that night, Rev. Foreman said, "My mother told me she thought I could do it. And the right hand did it!"

The church—the entire body of Christ from every race and nation—can learn from this motivational message of Rev. George Foreman, who has an astounding and inspirational record of 73 wins, 4 losses, and 68 knockouts. Every win, loss, and knockout provided priceless lessons that brought Rev. Foreman closer to fulfilling his destiny. It could have gone the other way, however, if Foreman had given up in his spirit.

Rev. George Foreman turned the sports world upside down by preparing himself mentally and spiritually for 20 long years for just one moment in time—one knockout punch that rang out around the entire world.

If he never wins a boxing match again, it doesn't even matter because he has already set a precedent. Now no one can say that it is impossible for someone over 40 and not in their prime to become the heavyweight champion of the world. His example becomes a major motivating force to all people who are concerned about personal development and achievement.

As believers from every racial, social, and economic background, we must begin to prepare ourselves to be used of God to give the devil and his demons a black eye and knock them out of our communities.

Ephesians 6:12 clearly tells us:

For we wrestle not against flesh and blood, but against principalities, against powers, against the ruler of the darkness of this world, against spiritual wickedness in high places.

Rev. Foreman fought against a human opponent with flesh, blood, and bones. The church's fight of faith is against the forces of satan and fallen angels who hate the very mention of the name of Jesus.

The battle is the Lord's, but we are His hands, arms, legs, and feet. We are the body of Christ, the army of God. In other words, it is His battle, but we are His soldiers on the frontline. So get ready for war against the devil.

Like Rev. Foreman, we need to pray, plan, and be patient and persistent so we can have a measurable, lasting impact and truly make a difference in the world. This is what walking through the doorway of destiny is all about—making a difference in your sphere of influence for the cause of Jesus Christ.

Learning to Walk

God wants His children to walk through the everyday, ordinary doorways of destiny. God wants us to grow and go through the various developmental stages of life whether we are a boxer, a baby, or a bloodwashed believer.

Yolanda, my precious little daughter of destiny, has grown tremendously since she was first born in January 1994. Three of her front teeth have come in, and, a few months ago, Yolanda completely elated me when she uttered her first words, "Da Da."

Brenda, however, was not too pleased when Yolanda said, "Da Da, Da Da, Da Da," all day long.

Brenda said to Yolanda, "I was the one who carried you for nine long months, baby girl."

After much coaxing, Yolanda finally said those precious words, "Ma Ma," to Brenda's delight.

We watched in wonder as Yolanda learned to sit in her high chair, hold her own bottle, and then try to take the spoon and bowl away from Brenda and me in an attempt to feed herself.

Before we knew it, Yolanda was wheeling around the house in her walker, traveling recklessly through the living room to her bedroom and to the kitchen. Even more amazing was the day she took her first step and began to walk toward us without anyone or anything supporting her. Now that's progress!

As these various developmental stages of infancy open right before our eyes at home, it makes me realize how delighted our heavenly Father must be when we begin to progress in our walk with Him. The Lord wants the church to grow spiritually, day by day.

Infancy, adolescence, preteens, the teenage years, young adulthood, middle age, and old age are all developmental stages of real life in the natural. The spiritual developmental stages—experiencing the new birth, receiving the baptism in the Holy Spirit, practicing the fruit of the Spirit, growing in grace, sanctification, and eternal life—are the divine doorways of destiny that the Master wants us to walk through and benefit from.

Behold, the Lord has set before you an open door, a new opportunity to grow, a developmental stage, and a doorway of destiny, and no man can close it.

If God divinely opens a door for you to preach in Africa, Asia, China, Europe, or Russia, and you have never ministered there before, that is certainly a new developmental stage in the growth of your outreach ministry. It is an open door, a doorway of destiny.

Like a little baby, new Christians don't learn to walk overnight. You have to crawl toward destiny first before you can even attempt to walk through the door. It took Rev. George Foreman 20 years to regain the title of Heavyweight Championship of the World, but he did it. He fulfilled that aspect of his destiny.

I encourage you not to despise reading the Scriptures, praying at mid-week service, singing a solo, introducing the preacher, carrying his briefcase, cleaning the church kitchen, or sweeping and mopping the floor.

The main point is God wants us to grow in Christ. He does not want us to remain stagnant. We should not be at the same place spiritually today that we were last week, last month, or last year.

The Five-Fold Ministry

God has given the church a five-fold ministry to provide dynamic spiritual leadership for believers in Jesus Christ. This ministry consists of five different types of gospel preachers: the apostle, prophet, evangelist, pastor, and teacher:

And he gave some, apostles; and some, prophets; and some, evangelists; and some, pastors and teachers; For the perfecting of the saints, for the work of the ministry, for the edifying of the body of Christ:

Till we all come in the unity of the faith, and of the knowledge of the Son of God, unto a perfect man, unto the measure of the stature of the fulness of Christ: That we henceforth be no more children, tossed to and fro, and carried about with every wind of doctrine, by the sleight of men, and cunning craftiness, whereby they lie in wait to deceive;

But speaking the truth in love, may grow up into him in all things, which is the head, even Christ: From whom the whole body fitly joined together and compacted by that which every joint supplieth, according to the effectual working in the measure of every part, maketh increase of the body unto the edifying of itself in love (Ephesians 4:11–16).

The purpose of this five-fold ministry is to build up the saints and to equip the body of Christ for the work of the ministry. All apostles, prophets, evangelists, pastors, and teachers have this distinct responsibility to work on the perfection—the holistic improvement—of the saints until the entire church comes together in the unity of the faith and an intimate awareness of the Son of God.

These five uniquely chosen preachers are spiritual coaches whose goal is to help the church grow through daily developmental stages in order for the church to walk through daily doorways of destiny. Their purpose is to make carnal, backsliding, backbiting, back–stabbing, and not-concerned-one-bit-about-holiness believers spiritually conformed, totally changed, and transformed. How? Through daily discipline and motivation, they will develop into a perfect man, unto the measure of the stature of the fullness of Christ.

The Master of Destiny, the Creator, our Blessed Redeemer, Jesus, God's own Son, calls the entire church—regardless of race, color, or creed—to be henceforth no more like children, "tossed to and fro, and carried about with every wind of doctrine" (Ephesians 4:14).

Whether you are a boxing preacher, deacon, or trustee; whether you are a baby Christian spiritually; or whether you are an older, more mature and seasoned believer who just sits in the pews, God still wants you to grow up in Him in all things, in every area of your life–even in those secret places that no one knows about.

You may have been saved for 25 years but have a serious problem that holds you back from fulfilling your personal destiny. No matter what the problem is, God wants us to admit it so we can continue to grow and receive help. He wants to "sanctify and cleanse it [the church] with the washing of water by the word" (Ephesians 5:26).

Success is getting up one more time.

Chapter 5

Destiny Before the Cradle to the Grave and Beyond

"The highest reward for a person's toil is not what they get for it, but what they become by it."–John Ruskin

Before the womb and until we get to heaven, God constantly opens doors for His children to walk through–to grow, develop, and utilize the unlimited resources of His eternal kingdom as revealed on earth.

Before Jeremiah was born, God had already ordained him to be a prophet to the nations.

Before I formed thee in the belly I knew thee; and before thou cameth forth out of the womb I sanctified thee, and I ordained thee a prophet unto the nations (Jeremiah 1:5).

Destiny is God's plan, or prophecy, for your life. To accomplish His purposes, God will open preordained opportunities for you to do a monumental work for His glory.

Jesus, the Anointed One, in His model prayer, better known to us as The Lord's Prayer, said:

Thy kingdom come. Thy will be done in earth, as it is in heaven (Matthew 6:10).

In other words, the will of God, the destiny of God, must be done on earth because it is already an established fact in the mind of God in heaven. That is why the apostle Paul wrote:

Let this mind be in you, which was also in Christ Jesus (Philippians 2:5).

The church needs a positive, Christ-centered attitude, a made-up mind that is willing to go all the way in the struggle of the last-day saints.

When insurmountable odds are strategically stacked against you by satan himself, and when your daily existence seems more like an elevator stuck on ground level zero, God is still able to deliver you and grant you the grace to walk victoriously through your personal doorway of destiny. He will help you overcome every single setback devised by the devil to defeat, demolish, and utterly destroy you.

The reason for discovering your divine destiny, for finding the mind of Christ, is to blow up the devil's plan to ruin your walk with God.

Old-Fashioned Knee-ology

The church actually stands on the shoreline with divine destiny in the distance, and God still beckons the church to launch out into the deep. The church does not need shallow-watered faith and a compromised Christianity.

As believers, we need to leave the safe, shallow cove of mediocrity and launch out into the deep waters of destiny where we can enjoy an intimate, passionate love affair with the Lord Jesus Christ.

An ankle-high, religious, tip-toe-through-the-tulips repertoire won't satisfy the church's dire need to survive in the troubled waters of a modern, high-tech society that doesn't want to hear anything about walking with God. A knee-high song and dance won't usher the Shekinah glory of God into our churches.

What will do the job? Old-fashioned knee-ology, the study of God down on our knees in fervent intercessory prayer, praise, and worship; that's what will invoke the waters of the Holy Spirit to rise higher and higher until the floodgates, the windows of heaven, and the doorways of destiny open up and pour out bountiful blessings.

Waist-deep theology, shoulder-length philosophy, and neck-high, man-made solutions won't meet the standards required of the church, by God Himself, to finish the course that leads to the doorways of destiny. Only as we step through the threshold can we promote positive change in our troubled communities.

Passing on the Torch

Dr. Francis A. Schaeffer, in his book, *The Church at the End of the Twentieth Century,* raised the question, "Does the church have a future in our generation?" He answered this way:

> I believe the church is in real danger. It is in for a rough day. We are facing present pressures and a future manipulation that will be so overwhelming in the days to come that they will make the battles of the last 40 years look like child's play.[2]

The church must launch out into the deep waters of destiny—where the fish are, where the people are—if we truly want to change the constant mishaps of our church ministries and actually minister to the misery of the jobless, homeless, hopeless, and hurting masses throughout the land.

As a people of destiny, we must also strongly consider investing in the next generation—our babies, children, preteens, teenagers, and young adults. These various age groups represent the next generation of leadership, and it is up to the church family to train as many of them as possible. Each of these groups has its own needs, and, as we minister to them, we must be aware of those particular needs.

One way for the church not to end up in child's play in the future is to train the next generation of leadership right now. Why? So the mistakes of the past are not repeated.

Only when we reach out to the next generation can we truly walk in the light of the prophecy that the church's greatest days are ahead. Why? Because youth play an important role in the fulfillment of that particular prophecy. If we leave them out, we take the chance of losing the vast benefits of that prophecy for the local church.

No longer can we push youth to the side because they truly are the next generation of leadership. Youth are a vital part of this "Walking Through the Doorway of Destiny" message, for without youth there is no future. I'll put it plain, and simple: No youth means no future church.

Anyone who has read the book of Revelation knows that the church will survive and the gates of hell will not succeed against it. That doesn't mean, however, that every individual church will survive. In some churches, the majority of members are all near the end of their journey, and there is no one to whom to pass the torch.

Just as Moses mentored Joshua for future leadership, we must train the next generation even before they are born. Moses trained Joshua through the power of a Spirit-led, disciplined life and then passed the torch on to the next generation of leadership.

We must not wait until our young people are 20, 25, 30, or 35, and say, "It's your turn to run the ship."

Reaching the next generation for Jesus Christ is essential in a world where young people are often pushed aside and their issues remain on the back-burner.

Good and Bad Seed

We must begin to train our children even while they are in their mother's womb. This is done by speaking to the unborn child and telling him that he is called, chosen, and predestined for greatness by the Creator. We must let the unborn baby know, "Even if the world calls you a mistake, you are not a mistake in God's eyes—you are a child of destiny and purpose."

After the child is born, we must continue to plant the positive message of the Master of Destiny in his spirit. Even before he can talk, we must read to him, sing to him, and teach him through example. These steps lay the foundation for future success.

If you are constantly cursing, smoking, stealing, drinking, taking drugs, and fighting when the baby is still in the mother's womb, and continue to do so as the child grows up, you are planting a bad seed whether you know it or not.

If you sow a seed of sexual, physical, and verbal child abuse, look out! Unless they receive deliverance from God, your children will grow up to be angry, selfish, violent, and cruel.

The American Psychiatric Glossary describes an abused child this way:

> A child or infant who has suffered repeated injuries, which may include bone fractures, neurologic and psychological damage, and sexual abuse at the hands of a parent, parents, or parent surrogates. The abuse takes place repeatedly and is often precipitated, in the case of physical abuse, by the child's minor and normally irritating behavior. Child abuse also includes child neglect.[3]

Child abuse, spousal abuse, family abuse, sexual abuse, and verbal abuse are arch enemies of divine destiny. Only God, through the power of the Holy Spirit, can destroy that yoke of bondage and break that generational curse.

If we don't invest in the next generation, destiny won't be fulfilled. If we don't specifically teach our children who they are in Christ, they will not grow to reach their generation for Christ in a rough world.

The modern-day church's clothing is wrinkled and spotted with the stain of neglect toward the next generation. Jesus is coming back for a glorious church without spot or wrinkle. We must clean up this mess first and then press it out if we expect the church to be prepared for Christ's return.

Reaching Generation X

With all the major ministries in the world today, only a handful care about reaching the next generation for Jesus Christ. In order for true revival to break out, we must change our attitudes toward the next generation—better known today as "Generation X."

You may not personally like Bible-based Christian rap and contemporary Christian music, but if it reaches young people for Jesus Christ, what is more important—their soul or your tradition?

You may not like their haircuts or style of clothes, but their soul is more important than those superficial things. Every adult man must take a younger man under his wing. Every adult woman must mentor a young woman and begin to invest in her life in order to reach the next generation and fulfill divine destiny.

Joel 2:28,29 states how the Holy Spirit desires to bridge the gap between the generations:

> And it shall come to pass afterward, that I will pour out my spirit upon all flesh; and your sons and your daughters shall prophesy, your old men shall dream dreams, your young men shall see visions: And also upon the servants and upon the handmaids in those days will I pour out my spirit.

Tell young people about your failures as well as your achievements. Tell them about the hard-core realities and jagged edges of life. Most of all, tell them Who Jesus is. Let the next generation know that you have been tempted and tried in the fire, but the Lord delivered you and opened doors for you.

Teach them that God's Word is true, and pass on what you have learned in life, as wise King Solomon did:

> Remember now thy Creator in the days of thy youth, while the evil days come not, nor the years draw nigh, when thou shalt say, I have no pleasure in them (Ecclesiastes 12:1).

This is how we reach the next generation—by investing in them. Teach them these three simple steps that a young person can take to fulfill his or her destiny:

1. Put God first in everything you do.

2. Don't wait until you are in trouble to call on God. Speak to Him every day through prayer.

3. Live life to its fullest in Christ Jesus.

The next generation is a vital doorway of destiny. In fact, they are our only hope for spreading the gospel once we are dead and gone. If we don't train them right now in the way that they should go concerning financial integrity, interpersonal relationships, spiritual maintenance, and plain old responsibility, we are in store for real trouble.

Concerning the destiny of the generations, the writer of Psalm 90:1,2 says:

> Lord, thou hast been our dwelling place in all generations. Before the mountains were brought forth, or ever thou hadst formed the earth and the world, even from everlasting to everlasting, thou art God.

God chose us before the foundation of the earth was laid—and that includes every juvenile delinquent, every honor student, and every high school dropout. God is no respecter of persons. He wants us to get our lives together by realizing the wealth of potential that lies dormant within our body, soul, and spirit.

Today's youth represent an open door to take the gospel to another level. Their energy and innovative genius is an asset—not a liability—the church needs to tap into.

Learn to listen to teenagers and young adults. They can tell you all about the drug deals, the big fights, and the latest gangs, and they know what it takes to reach them. One of the greatest weapons that the church has in its arsenal is youth on the move for Jesus Christ.

The apostle Paul wrote to young Timothy and said:

> Let no man despise thy youth; but be thou an example of the believers, in word, in conversation, in charity, in spirit, in faith, in purity (1 Timothy 4:12).

In an interview with *Charisma* magazine, evangelist Shirley Caesar said, "Our youth desperately need to know how special they are. Drugs and sexual promiscuity are stealing our kids, and we need to teach them to stand for who they are."

Mid-Life Crisis

Another crisis point along life's journey comes at the halfway mark. At the mid-life crisis stage, people begin to reevaluate their lives and think about the possibility of death.

King David wrote concerning his personal destiny:

> I have been young, and now am old; yet have I not seen the righteous forsaken, nor his seed begging bread (Psalm 37:25).

That is a scriptural example and excellent definition of destiny—God's prophecy concerning our personal lives before the cradle to the grave and beyond. People don't like talking about death because deep down in their hearts, they know they are not living life to its fullest and they are not fulfilling their divine destiny.

The Bible clearly says that the Lord will satisfy us with long life if we abide by His word.

Honour thy father and thy mother: that thy days may be long upon the land which the Lord thy God giveth thee (Exodus 20:12).

Psalm 91:16 states:

With long life will I satisfy him, and shew him my salvation.

God wants us to live a full, satisfied life. If it is not our time to die, we can fight by faith and live a little while longer. When it is God's actual appointed time, we can boldly declare, "When I walk through the valley of the shadow of death, I will fear no evil for the Master of Destiny is with me."

The apostle Paul did not fear death. He asked:

O death, where is thy sting? O grave, where is thy victory? (1 Corinthians 15:55).

When you are on the Lord's side, you don't have to fear the devil because your soul doesn't belong to him. The only valid reason to live a long life is to fulfill destiny concerning you, your family, and your church, and by being a witness for the Lord to the world.

Ecclesiastes 12:13,14 sums up this truth:

Let us hear the conclusion of the whole matter: Fear God, and keep his commandments: for this is the whole duty of man. For God shall bring every work into judgment, with every secret thing, whether it be good, or whether it be evil.

It takes a lifetime of developing and nurturing relationships with ordinary people, and having a great time in the process, to complete our mission in life-better known in this book as our personal destiny. You must live life to its fullest, and you must live as long as possible in order to be ready to die and know that you did the job God created you for.

When the Job is Done

The apostle Paul wrote:

For to me to live is Christ, and to die is gain (Philippians 1:21).

Paul realized that to be absent from the body is to be present with the Lord (2 Corinthians 5:8).

Every day we need to write our own eulogies by being true Christians who are concerned about the plight and chaos of our children and our communities. King Solomon stated that there is "a time to be born, and a time to die" (Ecclesiastes 3:2).

What is the reason for having a sense of divine destiny here on earth? To get people to realize that God wants to build His kingdom in the hearts of people, like it is already built in heaven, and get us ready for eternity with Jesus.

King Solomon went as far as to say that greater is "the day of death than the day of one's birth" (Ecclesiastes 7:1).

Why is the day of our death better than the day of our birth? Because the day of our death, as appointed by God and not before then, is the only day in which destiny can be completed 100 percent.

There are some aspects of my destiny that I have fulfilled, and some that I have failed to accomplish. But I will reach the potential point of a total 100 percent only when I come to the end of my journey. I love heaven, but I am not homesick for it yet because I know I still have some work to do here on earth.

The essence of destiny is best described through the analogy of the birthing process. The long haul over a lifetime fulfillment of destiny, however, can only be completed and determined by God when we take our last breath. Everyone has to be ready to die when it is his or her God-ordained time. If anything tries to knock you off before then, you must fight the good fight of faith against it.

Ready to Die?

Enoch had a tremendous testimony—he "walked with God: and he was not; for God took him" (Genesis 5:24; Hebrews 11:5). It pays to walk closely with God even when the pressure is on.

The prophet Elijah had such a keen sense of divine destiny that God did not even let him wait to die. He translated him instantly and took him to heaven in a chariot of fire.

God let Enoch and Elijah walk through heavenly doorways of destiny because they walked by faith, and not by sight.

King Solomon is also noted for saying:

Better is the end of a thing than the beginning thereof: and the patient in spirit is better than the proud in spirit (Ecclesiastes 7:8).

In other words, the fulfillment of destiny is even more important than the birth of destiny. Why? Because the fulfillment of destiny provides a solid testimony and example that gives vision to others for their future journey. (See Ecclesiastes 7:1.)

The reason we are born, then, is to get ready to die. A long life of destiny leaves a legacy of soul winning that changes the atmosphere and environment in which we live.

The apostle Paul declared:

I am ready not to be bound only, but also to die at Jerusalem for the name of the Lord Jesus (Acts 21:13).

Paul was ready to die, but it wasn't his appointed, predestined time.

After going to Jerusalem, Paul walked through many other doorways of destiny and even witnessed to the great King Agrippa, who could have killed him. Paul then journeyed back to Rome. He survived a shipwreck by floating on broken pieces of the boat. A venomous snake bit him, and yet he suffered no ill effects.

Why did Paul survive all of these earthly trials and tribulations? Because God still had some territory that He wanted Paul to snatch from the enemy. God wanted Paul to stay alive long enough to preach the gospel in the government and center of society and culture.

For what purpose? To lay the foundation for future generations to spread the gospel throughout the world and pass his vision on to the next generation. Paul had to continue to fight the good fight of faith until he finished his course as determined by God alone.

We must also learn to boldly declare, "I will live and not die until I have finished walking through every single doorway of destiny that God has set before me in this life."

Too many people are dying before their appointed date with divine destiny.

Change Your Destiny

In my community, the African-American community, life expectancy has dropped drastically in comparison to whites. Almost one-third of all Americans with AIDS and almost one-half of all children with AIDS are African-American. HIV death rates are three times higher in African-American males than in white men, and nine times higher among African-American women than in white women.

African-American males make up 80 percent or more of the prison population in most of our major cities and counties.

Whenever an economic recession takes place in the nation, an economic depression results in the black community. In fact, the Saturday, November 2, 1996 edition of the *New York Amsterdam News* states that ". . . 65 African Americans are diagnosed with HIV every day. If it continues to spread unchecked, by the year 2001, more than half of all Americans with AIDS will be black."

If we want to change our destiny, we must first acknowledge the facts in order to change them. Then we must stand on God's truth to turn them around one by one. That is not negative. That is addressing urban, hard-times, in-your-face reality by faith.

It's time for the church to wake up and smell the coffee. People are dying, and they are crying out right now for help for their wounded existence.

Suicide is not the answer to your heartaches. Sleeping pills and lethal injections are not the solution.

Using the rapture as an excuse not to work hard, instead of an essential teaching concerning the Bridegroom returning for His virgin bride, is not the answer. The rapture is an established matter of destiny. It will occur when the time is right, no matter what, and it is not a crutch for lazy Christians.

We must deal with the root of the problem, which is to distance ourselves from a philosophy of escapism and become a people of destiny who have their fingers on the pulse of the people. Why?

Because only then can we hear the voice of God clearly concerning the important issues of life—from the cradle to the grave and beyond.

Carman addressed this particular point in his book, *Raising The Standard*, when he wrote:

> Why should you want to buy a house if Jesus is coming back in a few short years or maybe a few months? Why go to college? Why prepare? Why have a savings account? Why prepare for the future or for your retirement? It is not as important that we know when He is coming as it is that we live our lives in the light of His coming. But that doesn't mean we put on robes and go up the hill. . . . If you are in school and you are preparing for a future, don't leave school. Prepare, because when He comes back, He is going to look and see who is faithful.[4]

Only Jesus Christ—Who is coming soon—the Everlasting Gentleman, Who keeps opening doors for His virgin bride, can make your life the masterpiece that it was meant to be before the dawn of time. But God expects us to work and prepare ourselves to be used by Him.

When you are on the Lord's side, you don't have to fear the devil because your soul doesn't belong to him.

Chapter 6

Destined to Do Greater Works

"Whether you think you can or think you can't–you are right"
–Henry Ford

When I first got saved, there was a heavy anointing upon my life, and I had a burden to fast and pray. Many days and nights I went to the old storage room in the back of the church and prayed.

Sometimes I prayed for an hour on my knees and skipped a meal. When I witnessed about Christ or prayed for the sick, God's anointing flowed like fresh oil–fresh oil, not a stale, ordinary, mundane, run-of-the-mill type of mentality; it was the anointing of the Holy Spirit.

When I came upon someone who was demon possessed, God gave me a spirit of discernment, and I cast out the demons in the authority and power of Jesus' name. I know for myself that prayer and fasting opens doors.

Destiny demands times in our lives when we must take a needed prayer and fasting hiatus. We need to break away from stale religion and recharge, revamp, and revitalize our relationship with God, the

Source of all life. It is also healthy to get away for a few days to gain a closer walk with Jesus.

People who don't pay this type of holy homage to God end up being incognito in their spiritual development. They hide and don't stand up for anything because they don't know who they are in Christ.

We can't walk though the doorways of destiny if we don't enrich our lives though the dynamic duo of fasting and prayer.

When the disciples wondered why they could not cast out a devil that possessed a young child, Jesus told them the reason:

> Because of your unbelief: for verily I say unto you, If ye have faith as a grain of mustard seed, ye shall say unto this mountain, Remove hence to yonder place; and it shall remove; and nothing shall be impossible unto you. Howbeit this kind goeth not out but by prayer and fasting (Matthew 17:20,21).

Too many Christians remain locked in the dungeons of disgrace and humiliation because of problems in their lives. Why? Because they lack the spiritual discipline for daily living that is developed only through fasting and prayer. Praying and fasting open doors for more effective ministry, which is one of the doorways of destiny.

Opening Doors of Opportunity

Having a burden to reach the lost, who have not heard the message of the Master, is the ultimate purpose of the doorway of destiny.

Acts 13 tells the story of two men, Barnabas and Saul (Paul), whom God called to do a predestined work for the kingdom. In order for their door of opportunity to be opened completely, the prophets and teachers of the church at Antioch had to fast and pray to hear the voice of the Father.

As they ministered to the Lord, and fasted, the Holy Ghost said, Separate me Barnabas and Saul for the work whereunto I have called them. And when they had fasted and prayed, and laid their hands on them, they sent them away. So they, being sent forth by the Holy Ghost, departed unto Seleucia; and from thence they sailed to Cyprus (Acts 13:2-4).

This open door to minister in Cyprus was Paul's first missionary journey. He would later write one-third of the entire New Testament.

God used two black men—Simeon, who was called Niger, and Lucius of Cyrene—along with Manaen, the foster brother of King Herod, to fast and pray and lay hands on and ordain Paul—a man who used to kill Christians. If these black men had not laid hands on their Jewish brother, one-third of the New Testament would be missing.

God wants the black man and the Jewish man to work together again. In fact, it was at this multi-ethnic congregation in Antioch that the disciples were first called Christians.

Then departed Barnabas to Tarsus, for to seek Saul: And when he had found him, he brought him unto Antioch. And it came to pass, that a whole year they assembled themselves with the church, and taught much people. And the disciples were called Christians first in Antioch (Acts 11:25,26).

This is a classic example of the essence of destiny. God requires that blacks, whites, Jews, Asians and all other races walk and work together in order to fulfill His plans and purposes in the earth.

A Man Whose Time Had Come

Pause for a moment, sit back wherever you are, and think about the wondrous works of the Miracle Worker named Jesus Christ of Nazareth.

When He came on the scene, Nathaniel sarcastically asked:

Can there any good thing come out of Nazareth? (John 1:46).

Jesus showed everyone through His life, death, and resurrection that He is the Best of the best. Jesus healed blind eyes, changed water to wine, walked on water, and miraculously fed the multitude with a few fish and loaves of bread.

Jesus was a man whose time had come, and, therefore, He could do things that no one else could imagine. Jesus Christ was and is fully God and yet fully man. Jesus Christ knew and still knows about all our troubles.

His ministry had such a tremendous impact upon the ancient and modern world that history is dated either A.D. or B.C.–after Christ's birth or before Christ's birth.

Think about the magnitude of Jesus' contributions of hope, healing, and essential wholeness that He provided to humanity. Then consider the astonishing fact that Jesus Christ actually said that we would do greater works than He.

What? Do greater works than Jesus? Yes, that is exactly what the Savior said!

Verily, verily, I say unto you, He that believeth on me, the works that I do shall he do also; and greater works than these shall he do; because I go unto my Father (John 14:12).

As you ponder that statement, it is only natural to wonder, "How can I do greater works than Jesus Christ Himself?"

Before we can answer, we must ask the next logical question: What were the works of ministry that Jesus Christ did in the first place?

Matthew 4:23 explains three specific works of ministry that Jesus Christ did on a regular basis:

And Jesus went about all Galilee, teaching in their synagogues, and preaching the gospel of the kingdom, and healing all manner of sickness and all manner of disease among the people.

These three ministry outreach activities sum up the vast scope of the brief earthly ministry of Jesus Christ of Nazareth as presented in the four gospels—Matthew, Mark, Luke, and John. Jesus Christ spent the majority of His precious time helping hurting and wounded people by teaching, preaching, and healing all types of sickness and disease.

Greater Than His Works?

If we are to do greater works than Jesus, then our teaching, preaching, and healing must be far greater than His. Any sane, rational person would respond that this is impossible and downright irreverent. Yet Jesus Christ Himself said that it would happen. Since Jesus said it, I affirm it and believe His Word.

You may say, "I haven't heard a teacher or preacher who was more profound than Jesus Christ. And I haven't seen any miracles or healings that compare to those wrought by the hands of the Master."

How then can we expect to do greater works than Jesus? For one simple reason: The Greater One lives in us.

When Jesus was born and wrapped in swaddling clothes and placed in a manger, He was one baby. When He grew up and eventually died for the sins of all humanity, He was one physical man. But when He rose again and sent the Holy Spirit, He decided to dwell in the hearts and minds of countless Christian believers, better known as the body of Christ.

Jesus Christ had the unrestricted anointing of the Holy Spirit upon Him so that He could do anything. We have the anointing of

the Holy Spirit only with measure because the glory would kill us if
we had it in full.

Since Jesus Christ, the Hope of Glory, lives in us, we can do the
greater works of teaching, preaching, and healing. Any sound Bible-
based teaching, preaching, and divine healing that occurs in our
individual ministries should be credited to Jesus Christ for He is the
One Who rose again and walked through the tomb door to change
our destiny.

We are only vessels to accomplish the greater works that God
desires. Therefore, we must boldly teach, preach, and practice Bible-
based messages of faith—and not double-minded sermons of doubt
and fear that ruin the development of destiny in our lives. We are
destined to do the greater works because we are the church, the
body of Christ, and the gates of hell will not prevail against us.

When Jesus Christ lived on earth, He resided in one body. Today,
however, Jesus Christ resides in the hearts of countless men and
women throughout the whole world. Yes, we are destined to do the
greater works of teaching, preaching, and healing, not by our might
or power, but by His Spirit.

According to 1 John 4:4:

> Ye are of God, little children, and have overcome them: because greater
> is he that is in you, than he that is in the world.

New Opportunities

Doing the greater works of Jesus Christ is also a matter of utiliz-
ing the modern technology and resources that were not available
when Jesus Christ walked the earth. Today we can literally preach,
teach, and release the healing power of God in Jesus' name to the
world through television, radio, satellites, cable, videotapes, audio

cassettes, CD-Rom, and other various forms of computer technology, as well as books such as this one.

This ability to utilize new technologies to preach, teach, and spread God's healing power is a fulfillment of Jesus Christ's prophecy concerning the church. Our Lord and Savior said:

Behold, I have set before thee an open door, and no man can shut it (Revelation 3:8).

Jesus Christ has placed an open door of new opportunities before us, and nobody can close it! The purpose of this doorway of destiny is to walk through it and declare His glory more effectively. The purpose of this doorway of destiny is to improve our service to the Master of Destiny while we are still on the embattled mission field of everyday life in a sinful world.

The purpose of this open door is to make us realize that the church, village, town, county, city, and state where God has placed us is our open door of opportunity to do the greater works that we were born to do.

Jeremiah 1:5 says:

Before I formed thee in the belly I knew thee; and before thou cameth forth out of the womb I sanctified thee, and I ordained thee a prophet unto the nations.

While we were yet in our mother's womb, we were destined to do the greater works of teaching, preaching, and divine healing.

Yes, we can do the greater works because Jesus Christ lives within our hearts through the presence of the Holy Spirit. We can preach, teach, and heal by God's power with all boldness. We can rebuild our communities. We can instill godly pride and help build self-esteem in our neighbors.

It is not by our might or power that we can make a lasting impact but only through the Holy Ghost-filled power of Jesus' name. Jesus Christ, the Prime Mover, the Destiny Shaper, the Greater One—that is Who He is.

> **Jesus Christ spent the majority of His precious time helping hurting and wounded people by teaching, preaching, and healing all types of sickness and disease.**

Chapter 7

Destined to Succeed

"The talent of success is nothing more than doing what you can do well, and doing well whatever you do"–Henry Wadsworth Longfellow

We have been called and chosen according to God's pre-established purpose. When we begin to understand God's purpose for our destiny, we can begin to move toward it. This is a learning and growing process that unfolds day by day.

As we get closer to the Master of our destiny, the revelation that all things work together for good for those individuals who love the Lord and are called according to His purpose becomes more than mere words. That statement is a fact.

And we know that all things work together for good to them that love God, to them who are the called according to his purpose. For whom he did foreknow, he also did predestinate to be conformed to the image of his Son, that he might be the firstborn among many brethren. Moreover whom he did predestinate, them he also called: and whom he called, them he also justified: and whom he justified, them he also glorified. What shall we then say to these things? If God be for us, who can be against us? (Romans 8:28–31).

What is God's purpose? That we walk through the doorway of destiny. That we fulfill His descriptive, specific, blow-by-blow agenda for life's journey every single step of the way.

For God:

Hath saved us, and called us with an holy calling, not according to our works, but according to his own purpose and grace, which was given us in Christ Jesus before the world began (2 Timothy 1:9).

In other words, we must learn to be happy with the fact that Jesus called us with a holy calling. Stop trying to be like someone else and learn to walk in the anointing of your own calling.

Why must you walk in the anointing of your own calling? Because it is impossible to fulfill destiny without the anointing. It is impossible to walk through any doorway of destiny, any godly door of opportunity, and not be in the Spirit. If you try to do that, you will mess up God's perfect plan for your agenda every time.

You may get to preach, teach, sing, and lay hands on the sick, but God's perfect plan will not be fulfilled. Why? Because when everyone else is in the Spirit, you will be in the flesh.

Our culture provides plenty of examples of preachers who suffer today because they played with the dice of destruction instead of walking through the doorways of destiny.

Isaiah 10:27 says:

And it shall come to pass in that day, that his burden shall be taken away from off thy shoulder, and his yoke from off thy neck, and the yoke shall be destroyed because of the anointing.

In other words, only the anointing destroys the yoke of bondage. The anointing does not break the yoke of bondage and addiction as many people have thought for many years. The anointing, however, does destroy, eliminate, and eradicate the yoke of deceptive bondage. If you break something, it can be fixed. But if you destroy it, it is gone.

All things do not work together for the good of many Christians because there is no anointing in their life.

They are trying to be a prophet, teacher, evangelist, pastor, or apostle, and God called them to be ordinary Christians. They are not happy because they don't realize that they are called with a holy calling.

We are called not according to titles or positions but according to God's purpose and grace. Too many people just want a title when what they need is a teacher—someone to train them to discover who they are in Christ.

Working Out For Good

Stephen was the first deacon in church history, but his ministry was just as powerful as most modern five-fold ministries. Why was this? Because he walked in the reality of his calling.

Even as he was being stoned to death for preaching the gospel, his eyes were gazing on heaven. As a Christian martyr, Stephen proved that all things work together for the good. Why? Because he loved the Lord and was called according to His purpose.

Saul of Tarsus, who sent out decrees to slay and slaughter Christians, was present at the execution of Stephen. Later, when Saul got saved on the Damascus road and changed his destiny, Jesus asked him:

Why persecutest thou me?... It is hard for thee to kick against the pricks (Acts 9:4,5).

Jesus wanted to know why Saul was opposing God's children.

What satan had intended for evil, God used as an opportunity to draw a sinner who despised the gospel of Jesus Christ.

All things do work together for the ultimate good of those who love the Lord and are called according to His purpose. God's Word does not say that all things work out the way that we want. But they do work out to the good, to our best advantage, if we are walking in the reality of our calling. When we do this, we are destined to succeed.

When Your Dreams Don't Make Sense

Joseph, the son of Jacob, was given a beautiful multi-colored robe by his father and was extremely self-confident as a youth. His brothers, however, grew jealous and bitter toward him and decided to do away with Joseph because he made the mistake of sharing his dreams of destiny with them.

> Now Israel loved Joseph more than his children, because he was the son of his old age: and he made him a coat of many colours. And when his brethren saw that their father loved him more than all his brethren, they hated him, and could not speak peaceably unto him. And Joseph dreamed a dream, and he told it to his brethren: and they hated him yet the more (Genesis 37:3–5).

It is not always wise to share your dreams of destiny with brothers and sisters in Christ who don't care about your future. It was part of destiny, however, for Joseph to tell his dreams because God was going to teach his brothers a lesson, even though this wouldn't occur until many years later.

In the meantime, the brothers conspired to kill him because they could not understand Joseph's dreams in which they and their parents bowed before him.

> And they said one to another, Behold, this dreamer cometh. Come now therefore, and let us slay him, and cast him into some pit, and we will say, Some evil beast hath devoured him: and we shall see what will become of his dreams (Genesis 37:19,20).

The same thing is happening today in many churches across the land. The anointing of the Holy Ghost cannot flow because brothers and sisters in Christ are more carnal minded than Christ minded. They are ready to throw anyone who gets in their way into the pit.

We must realize that not everyone who cries, "Lord, Lord" is really concerned about following the Lord. Yes, they may be saved and filled with the Holy Ghost, but they are not walking though the doorway of destiny.

As people of destiny, we cannot waste time with two-faced soldiers who will stab us in the back before we can raise the blood-stained banner for our Lord. Gone are the days when the church can gloss over its troubles.

A Man of Destiny

After Joseph's brothers tore off his coat of many colors, they did not kill him because their brother Reuben insisted he be allowed to live. Instead, they threw him into an empty pit with no water. When a caravan came by, they sold Joseph to the Ishmaelites for 20 pieces of silver. Once he arrived in Egypt, Joseph was sold again.

Even today–for the right price–many people are willing to say anything even if it isn't the truth.

The events that followed show how God can work out all things, even bad situations, to our ultimate good.

And Joseph was brought down to Egypt; and Potiphar, an officer of Pharaoh, captain of the guard, an Egyptian, bought him of the hands of the Ishmeelites, which had brought him down thither. And the Lord was with Joseph, and he was a prosperous man; and he was in the house of his master the Egyptian.

And his master saw that the Lord was with him, and that the Lord made all that he did prosper in his hand. And Joseph found grace in his sight, and he served him: and he made him overseer over his house, and all that he had he put into his hand.

And it came to pass from the time that he had made him overseer in his house, and over all that he had, that the Lord blessed the Egyptian's house for Joseph's sake; and the blessing of the Lord was upon all that he had in the house, and in the field. And he left all that he had in Joseph's hand; and he knew not ought he had, save the bread which he did eat. And Joseph was a goodly person, and well favoured (Genesis 39:1–6).

What Joseph's brothers had intended for evil, God brought some good out of it. The experience of being sold into slavery in Egypt was actually a doorway of destiny for Joseph.

Joseph was destined to succeed. Why? Because he walked in the revelation of his calling in one accord with God's ultimate purpose.

Potiphar realized that Joseph was a man of destiny because everything Joseph did prospered. The Lord also blessed Potiphar's house because Joseph, a man of destiny, was staying there.

When men and women of divine destiny are present, success is inevitable. When individuals have the leading of the Spirit operating in their lives, everything they do flows from the anointing and brings blessing to others.

After Potiphar's wife tried to seduce Joseph and then lied about what had happened, her husband put Joseph in jail. When Joseph ran away from Potiphar's wife, he had to run away naked—but God provided a way of escape.

When you are cornered in the time of temptation, look for the door because God will always provide some way of escape. You don't have to sleep with the enemy and delay destiny for decades and generations.

If you have sinned, run to the altar and repent right now. You may have destroyed some things that were meant to be, but do not despair. You can pick up the broken pieces and finish all that you can to the glory of God.

The Journey to Destiny

While in prison, Joseph interpreted the dreams of the butcher and the baker, which opened the door to Pharaoh's court. There, Joseph even interpreted Pharaoh's dreams, which meant that Egypt would have seven years of prosperity followed by seven years of famine.

Like any true person of destiny, Joseph was destined to succeed because all things do work together for the good of those who love the Lord and are called according to His purpose.

Read how Pharaoh responded to Joseph's prophetic interpretation of his dreams:

And Pharaoh said unto his servants, Can we find such a one as this is, a man in whom the Spirit of God is? And Pharaoh said unto Joseph, Forasmuch as God hath shewed thee all this, there is none so discreet and wise as thou art: Thou shalt be over my house, and according unto thy word shall all my people be ruled: only in the throne will I be greater than thou.

And Pharaoh said unto Joseph, See, I have set thee over all the land of Egypt. And Pharaoh took off his ring from his hand, and put it upon Joseph's hand, and arrayed him in vestures of fine linen, and put a gold chain about his neck: And he made him to ride in the second chariot which he had; and they cried before him, Bow the knee: and he made him ruler over all the land of Egypt.

And Pharaoh said unto Joseph, I am Pharaoh, and without thee shall no man lift up his hand or foot in all the land of Egypt (Genesis 41:38–44).

Joseph was destined to succeed because God was on his side. God took Joseph on a journey to destiny from his father Jacob's house to the pit, to Potiphar's house, to jail, to Pharaoh's side.

If God is for us, He is greater than the world against us.

All things do work together for good if we trust in God. Of course, Joseph's success did not happen overnight. Joseph could have given up in the pit or in the bedroom or in jail, but instead he persevered on his journey to destiny.

He knew that God had opened a door for him that no man, not even his brothers, could shut. In the end, God used the seven-year harvest and the seven-year famine to fulfill Joseph's dream of destiny—his prophecy that his family would bow before him. No one could deny that God was in control of Joseph's ultimate destiny.

The Last Word

Our daily decisions determine our daily destiny. Common sense—and the Scriptures—make it clear that our choices affect our future. When it comes to divine providence, however, God makes the final decision. Why? Because He must have the preeminence, glory, and the honor—and not man. God always gets the last word.

Such was the case with Joseph's brothers. They didn't care about destiny, and they didn't care about Joseph, but God cared.

Why was Joseph destined to succeed? Let me give you four reasons:

1. His success was part of God's predestined plan.

2. He was called by God based upon His predestined plan and purpose.

3. He was justified. Joseph walked uprightly before God with an attitude of true humility.

4. He knew that his mortal body would be glorified when the trumpet sounds and the dead in Christ rise.

God caused Joseph's brothers, who had sold him into slavery, to come before him for food in the time of great famine. Read how Joseph handled the situation:

And Joseph said unto his brethren, Come near to me, I pray you. And they came near. And he said, I am Joseph your brother, whom ye sold into Egypt. Now therefore be not grieved, nor angry with yourselves, that ye sold me hither: for God did send me before you to preserve life.

For these two years hath the famine been in the land: and yet there are five years in the which there shall neither be earing nor harvest. And God sent me before you to preserve you a posterity in the earth, and to save your lives by a great deliverance.

So now it was not you that sent me hither, but God: and he hath made me a father of Pharaoh, and lord of all his house, and a ruler throughout all the land of Egypt (Genesis 45:4–8).

It pays to serve God.

A Race Within Itself

Like Joseph the dreamer, who was destined to succeed, the Christian church must not be controlled by the government or sleep with the enemies of truth. Of course, we must vote and be involved with federal, state, and local government but not controlled by it.

Evil abounds when good men sit idly by and let unqualified individuals who don't love the Lord govern a land that was founded on Christian principles. American atrocities such as slavery, Jim Crow, and segregation are glaring examples of how America began to stray from God's perfect will.

When school prayer ended in 1962, the process continued to rot the very foundations of our nation. Suicide increased; homicide increased; child abuse increased; rape and incest increased. Sin abounded because good men and women sat idly by while atheists decided to destroy any acknowledgment of God in the public schools. In essence, America said, "We don't need to follow God."

Our voice and our vote must be heard because they determine our destiny and the political landscape. We must not take the power of the ballot for granted.

Why not? Just ask Nomaza Paintin, the niece of African National Congress leader Nelson Mandela, who was the first non-white person to vote in the historic 1994 South African first all-race election. She cast her absentee ballot at the Justice Department of New Zealand, and the time difference caused her to vote one day ahead of the actual election.

Ask the new President of South Africa, Nelson Mandela, the freedom fighter who was imprisoned for 27 years, and Arch Bishop Desmond Tutu, and the economically blighted black people of the struggle in South Africa who voted for the very first time in their lives. Just ask the 108-year-old black woman who, days after voting, said, "Now I can die in peace."

Our South African friends would tell us not to take the ballot—a literal door of opportunity—for granted. God has set an open door before them, and no man can close it.

Even in America, many people who were slaves and second class citizens shed their blood so that every citizen of this nation could have the right to vote.

You might ask, "What does this have to do with the development of my faith and destiny?"

Everything. These examples of endurance of faith held under a knife of racism and pure hatred show that we, as Christians, can also overcome insurmountable odds if we stick together as one body in Christ—regardless of race, creed, or color.

Our Lord and Savior Jesus Christ is not coming back for the black church, the white church, the Asian church, or the Jewish church. Jesus is coming back for a glorious church without spot or wrinkle. This glorious church is a race within itself made up of all the races in the entire world.

When men and women of divine destiny are present, success is inevitable.

Chapter 8

Walking Through the Doorway of Destiny

"If a man is called to be a streetsweeper, he should sweep streets even as Michelangelo painted, or Beethoven composed music, or Shakespeare wrote poetry. He should sweep streets so well that all the hosts of heaven and earth will pause to say, here lived a great streetsweeper who did his job well."–Dr. Martin Luther King, Jr.

Many of us have not heard what the Spirit is saying to the church today. We have heard the preacher minister from great Bible texts, but within a given week or month, that is the only time some folks crack open their Bibles.

We must hear what the Spirit is saying to the churches and actually do it. We must not let this message go in one ear and out the other. From the pulpit to the pew, we must let God speak to the core of our being that there might be a revolution in our lives for Jesus Christ.

How many of us want to be radical for the cause of Christ? We look around the world, and we see people who are bold and radical for other causes–some we agree with and many we don't–but at least they are standing for something.

Some of our brothers and sisters are fighting against abortion-on-demand by marching in mass numbers. Others are actually willing to give their very lives for the cause, and their opponents on the other side of the issue are willing to do the same.

Those who march in behalf of causes such as AIDS, abortion, and substance abuse awareness are willing to give their time, talent, and very being. How many Christians do you know who are willing to stand up, speak up, and march toward the doorway of destiny concerning these perplexing issues of life?

The Lord is trying to speak to the church, and He wants us to listen and get our marching orders from the Master. As blood-washed believers, we must discover the true meaning of the message and mission, as well as correct the misdirection of the church in our sphere of influence. God is calling us to get into right relationship with Him. Why? Because the Lord hates religion, but He loves Christianity in action.

If one person with a sense of divine destiny is dangerous to the works of darkness, imagine what a whole army of believers could do. As we submit to something bigger than ourselves, something very special happens.

Corporate Destiny

When we begin to personalize this revelation of divine destiny, the blessings no longer have only individual impact. When Christians who are pursuing their destiny come together in praise and worship, God showers down a corporate blessing from the portals of glory.

The fulfillment of our personal destiny is precious in the eyes of God. We have no hope of attaining any type of corporate destiny without the foundation of personal destinies that are nurtured and unified through the blood of the Lamb.

We need to hear from God personally before we can bless the corporate body of Christ. We need to hear God's voice in our lonely valleys before we can shout it to everyone from the mountain top.

God designed the fulfillment of personal destiny to be the launching pad of corporate destiny. God did not speak to Moses at the burning bush to soothe his ego. God spoke to Moses to prepare him to lead a corporate body, the children of Israel, out of bondage.

God did not blind Saul, the persecutor of the church, on the road to Damascus just for the fun of it. God had in mind the corporate destiny of the entire New Testament church. Seeing the church down through the generations, God knew those of us alive today would read the New Testament, one-third of which was written by the apostle Paul.

See the Big Picture

Our personal destiny is extremely important. But remember that personal destiny is worthless if you don't care about the big picture. Instead of focusing on yourself, expand your vision to include the corporate destiny of your local church. God speaks to our hearts regarding personal destiny only because He intends it to impact the life of a corporate body in some way. After we have begun to pursue our personal destiny, we can't forget about the corporate destiny of our church. Many older saints understood their identity as a corporate people, which is reflected in this song:

Walk together children. Don't you get weary.
Pray together children. Don't you get weary.
Sing together children. Don't you get weary.
For there is a great camp meeting in the Promised Land.

You will never be all God desires you to be if you don't support a Holy Spirit-led local church and respect God's undershepherd who leads that flock. The realization of your destiny is linked to your support of God's program in the local church and His mouthpiece: the pastor, teacher, prophet, evangelist, or apostle.

Timothy could not fulfill his destiny without the training he received from the apostle Paul. Joshua could not fulfill his destiny without the lessons he learned from Moses. Elisha could not receive a double portion of the anointing without constantly undergirding the ministry of Elijah.

I am not talking about supporting some crooked, grandiose, self-centered man or woman who does not care about feeding the sheep and seeing them fulfill their personal and corporate destiny. Men and women of destiny support God's program, plan, and vision in the local church. Men and women of destiny give up their own desires and invest in the God-ordained vision of their pastor.

Your personal ministry will never be any stronger than your support of your pastor and local church. Remember this biblical principle of success. God opens doorways of destiny for those who are faithful to His program.

If you really want your God-ordained vision of victory to become reality, then first invest in the vision of a true man or woman of God. Even Jesus didn't do His own thing, but He did the will of His Father. Then and only then will God open doors in your life and your personal ministry that no man can close.

The Door-Way

God wants us to know Him in an intimate, close manner. God wants us to know Him so closely that we end up giving birth to destiny in every area of our life. This must happen so that we can tell the members of our various communities that we have found a Savior. Through His power, we can actually make a difference.

God has a doorway of destiny that He wants each and every one of us to walk though. The Master of Destiny desires for His bride, the church, to forsake the peripheral edges of compromise and mediocrity and walk throughout the household of God's kingdom.

As believers we must not only sit on the steps or rest on the porch. We must walk through the doorway. We are called to:

Enter into his gates with thanksgiving, and into his courts with praise (Psalm 100:4).

Once we are in the household, we will discover there are many rooms and opportunities for growth inside.

Now therefore ye are no more strangers and foreigners, but fellowcitizens with the saints, and of the household of God; And are built upon the foundation of the apostles and prophets, Jesus Christ himself being the chief corner stone; In whom all the building fitly framed together groweth unto an holy temple in the Lord: In whom ye also are builded together for an habitation of God through the Spirit (Ephesians 2:19–22).

Jesus is the chief cornerstone of the building of God. Jesus is also our architect, our brick mason, our general contractor, and He sits at the right hand of the chairman of the eternal board of trustees. Jesus Christ truly is our all and all.

The psalmist was correct when he wrote:

Except the Lord build the house, they labour in vain that build it (Psalm 127:1).

Where the Journey Begins

God the Father wants us to walk through the doorway of destiny because Jesus Christ, His only begotten Son, is the Door. Jesus Himself said:

I am the door: by me if any man enter in, he shall be saved, and shall go in and out, and find pasture (John 10:9).

Jesus Christ is not only the One who gives us new opportunities for growth, but Jesus is also the Road, the Highway, the Door of opportunity to get saved, healed, reclaimed, recharged, revived, and delivered.

Anyone who has received salvation since the resurrection of Christ has to come to God the Father through the name of Jesus. There is only one way to find true and lasting, eternal freedom, and that is through the Door of Life, Jesus Christ, the Savior of the world.

Jesus also said:

I am the way, the truth, and the life: no man cometh unto the Father, but by me (John 14:6).

Since Jesus Christ is the Door—the Only Way to the Father's arms of love, refuge, safety, and shelter—that makes Him the Door-Way Who can open doors that no man can close.

Walking through the doorway of destiny is not some figurative experience, but it is a literal and continuous journey, a right of passage. Once we walk through the door, we can explore the real possibilities that are presented because Jesus Christ has already made provision for their fulfillment.

Throughout our journey, Jesus is a Friend Who sticks closer than a brother. How does He do that? Through the presence of the Holy Spirit, the blessed paraclete, Who is called alongside to help, lead, and guide us.

Jesus Christ can direct our footsteps.

The steps of a good man are ordered by the Lord (Psalm 37:23).

Indecisive, double-minded Christians who do not follow the words of Jesus Christ and the prompting of the Holy Spirit are unstable and will get progressively worse if they continue to walk along that same path of destruction. When instability raises its ugly head, we must ask our heavenly Father for wisdom and the ability to use our knowledge correctly, effectively, and efficiently.

Behind the Three Doors

Churches are being destroyed from within because of a lack of knowledge concerning their sense of destiny and purpose. Where there is no direction, believers will be lost and left to wander aimlessly through the wilderness of life. They do not have the slightest clue concerning how to get back home and walk through the doorway of destiny.

Three doors are mentioned in the book of Revelation. Door number one is the "open door," the door of service.

> And to the angel of the church in Philadelphia write; These things saith he that is holy, he that is true, he that hath the key of David, he that openeth, and no man shutteth; and shutteth, and no man openeth; I know thy work: behold, I have set before thee an open door, and no man can shut it: for thou hast a little strength, and has kept my word, and has not denied my name (Revelation 3:7,8).

First, we must first come to our senses and admit our need to come back home to the center of God's will. Once we accept and acknowledge that we are incomplete without the direction of the Master of our destiny, we can then begin to walk toward the door that represents the totality of our potential.

Behind door number one are the doorways of our future with all of its faults and failures. Also included in this package is our testimony of how God brought us through the shark-infested waters and struggles of life.

Door number one also holds the reason why we believe in God, because without Him we would be nothing. The quality of our existence is directly dependent upon His presence in our midst.

Behind door number one, our heavenly Father looks down from the portals of glory at the predestined agenda that He wrote for our life. At the same time, He is clearing a path for us to succeed in life.

Finally, behind door number one is the Holy Spirit, Who is ready to be the latter rain that we need for the long-awaited, much-prophesied last days revival that will bring the church to its knees in humble submission to God.

Behind door number one are the doorways of destiny—everything we need to excel in this life, and everything we need to enjoy eternity with Jesus Christ our Lord.

According to Revelation 3:20, the second door is fellowship with Christ.

Behold, I stand at the door, and knock: if any man hear my voice, and open the door, I will come into him, and will sup with him, and he with me.

Behind door number two, Jesus Christ patiently knocks at the entrance of our hearts—even when we don't get up to answer the door. Jesus Christ also opens doors of opportunity for His children.

Revelation 4:1 mentions door number three:

After this I look, and, behold, a door was opened in heaven: and the first voice which I heard was as it were of a trumpet talking with me; which said, Come up hither, and I will shew thee things which must be hereafter.

The Christian believer has to walk through all three doors—the door of service, the door of fellowship, and the door of heaven—in order to finish the course of destiny. To begin, however, all you have to do is take the first step.

The Mystery Revealed

Why teach from the book of Revelation? Isn't it a mystery?

Yes, but for the believer who studies to show himself approved to God by rightly dividing the word of truth, Revelation is a mystery revealed.

The actual word "revelation" means to reveal, to enlighten. This revealed mystery tells us that—when all is said and done—Jesus and His army win. This book declares God's plan and purpose for our eternal destiny, a doorway that we must walk through.

The book of Revelation unfolds events that will surely come to pass. John the revelator wrote under the divine anointing of the Holy Spirit:

> Blessed is he that readeth, and they that hear the words of this prophecy, and keep those things which are written therein: for the time is at hand (Revelation 1:3).

Prophetic events, such as the rapture of the church, will occur no matter what.

That's why we need to get in line with God's program and be on the right side of destiny. A train of God's glory—and God's wrath—will sweep through the earth.

We better get ready and not miss this present visitation of God's glory because God is doing a new thing. It is not new to Him, but it is new to us. The Godhead knew about it before the foundations of the earth were established.

God is doing a new thing because the doors of communism have collapsed, and revival is occurring in Russia. The Berlin Wall has been broken down, and its huge stones are now symbols of newfound freedom for the residents of East and West Berlin. The doors of China are beginning to crack open to the gospel as never before.

God is doing a new thing because African Americans, who did not have the right to vote until 1966, are now leading major ministries that have multiracial outreaches and significant impact in the communities where they reside.

God is doing a new thing because women who were once relegated to staying behind the scenes are becoming modern day trailblazers for God, anointed preachers and teachers of the gospel of Jesus Christ.

The book of Revelation is in the Bible so we will get our own personal house in order before it's too late. God wants us to be part of what He is doing in the earth.

Getting Your House in Order

The overriding purpose of walking though the doorways of destiny is to create an environment of excellence by cleaning up the messy rooms of our lives. We need to go into our spiritual kitchen and make sure we have the fruit of the Spirit and the meat of the Word nourishing us. We need to throw out the stale, nasty, old garbage of false teaching that could smell up the house.

We have to go into our spiritual living room and dust away the cobwebs of wild lifestyles and vacuum up the dirt and residue of deception. We have to check our spiritual bathrooms to make sure the living water of the Holy Spirit is functioning at peak efficiency in our house.

Finally, we need to go into the spiritual bedroom to find out if the aroma of our praises is reaching and pleasing the Master.

We need to check ourselves to see if we are dressed for battle. Or is our armor—our helmet of salvation, breastplate of righteousness, belt of truth, sword of the Spirit, shield of faith, lance of prayer, and shoes of peace–strewn all over the floor?

It's time to get our house in order, and we must walk through the door in order to get into the house.

Setting Goals for Yourself

In these last days, things are changing, and our old formulas are not working. I can clearly hear the words of the Holy Spirit as recorded in Isaiah 43:18,19:

> Remember ye not the former things, neither consider the things of old. Behold, I will do a new thing; now it shall spring forth; shall ye not know it? I will even make a way in the wilderness, and rivers in the dessert.

God is not caught up in the traditions of man. Tradition holds back the manifold blessings of God in our lives. It does not matter how your father, mother, aunt, or uncle did it. God is saying, "Let Me deal with you and show you the divine direction and the doorways that I want you to walk through."

According to Galatians 5:25:

> If we live in the Spirit, let us also walk in the Spirit.

That is why Jesus Christ, the Master of the church, the Alpha and the Omega, gave a distinct mission and message to John the revelator on the Isle of Patmos.

> I John, who also am your brother, and companion in tribulation, and in the kingdom and patience of Jesus Christ, was in the isle that is called Patmos, for the word of God, and for the testimony of Jesus Christ. I was in the Spirit on the Lord's day, and heard behind me a great voice, as of a trumpet, Saying, I am Alpha and Omega, the first and the last: and, What thou seest, write in a book, and send it unto the seven churches which are in Asia; unto Ephesus, and unto Smyrna,

and unto Pergamos, and unto Thyatira, and unto Sardis, and unto Philadelphia, and unto Laodicea (Revelation 1:9–11).

John's divine assignment was to write messages to the seven churches of Asia Minor. The late civil rights leader, Rev. Dr. Martin Luther King, Jr., wrote of John the revelator, "Thank God for John who, centuries ago, caught a vision of the new Jerusalem. God grant that those of us who still walk the road of life will catch this vision and decide to move forward to that city of complete life in which the length and the breadth and the height are equal."[5]

God also yearns for us to take time to write about our hopes, aspirations, dreams, personal goals, and visions of victory. We should review these goals at least three times a day—one for the Father, one for the Son, and one for the Holy Ghost.

In writing our goals, we should literally chart the course of our destiny by the leading of the Holy Spirit. We must ask pertinent questions, such as: Where will I be one year from now? Five years from now? Or even 50 years from now?

Habakkuk 2:2 states:

And the Lord answered me, and said, Write the vision, and make it plain upon tables, that he may run that readeth it.

Your vision and mission statement for your life, your future, and your destiny should not be so complicated that you cannot make heads or tails of it, and no one else can figure out what you are talking about. When it comes to our long-term and short-term goals, we need to keep them plain, clear, and concise. By actually writing our goals, we are making a contract between ourselves and God to do His will.

The Church of the Open Door

What does Revelation 3:28 say?

I know thy works: behold, I have set before thee an open door, and no man can shut it: for thou hast a little strength, and hast kept my word, and hast not denied my name.

This verse is written to the church of Philadelphia. God saw their faithfulness and obedience to His word.

The church of Philadelphia was a successful church—not because they had money, riches, and fame, because they did not possess such luxuries. Their success did not result from their social, economic, or political status in the community. The church of Philadelphia would not be considered successful today according to the litmus test of many church growth seminars.

The church of Philadelphia was successful for one reason: When hell and high water rose, they still made God's desires their desires. Even when they were weak and frail in the eyes of many, they still believed God's Word that He is a Savior, Healer, and Deliverer, and they never denied the name of Jesus.

This is very important because Jesus Himself said:

But whosoever shall deny me before men, him will I also deny before my Father which is in heaven (Matthew 10:33).

Jesus also said to the church of Philadelphia, "I know thy works."

God is still saying to the church today, "I know your works. I know when you're praying. I know when you're fasting, and I know when you're fooling around and faking it."

God knows everything there is to know about us. We cannot trick God or pull one over on Him. God is omnipresent—He is everywhere at the same time. God is omnipotent—He possesses all power. God is omniscient—He has all knowledge and wisdom. The Lord God Jehovah knows the real deal all the time.

In honor of the Philadelphia church's humility, Jesus Christ designed an open door, a door of opportunity, a doorway of destiny to spread the gospel to those who hadn't heard it yet. No one could close this door and lock it because only Jesus Christ holds the key to the doorway of destiny. It is the Father's pleasure to give us the keys to the kingdom, but the master key belongs to Jesus.

Even in their apparent weakness, the church of Philadelphia still served the Lord in Spirit and in truth with their whole heart. Jesus, therefore, opened a doorway of destiny for them—and not for the six other churches of Asia Minor—because the Philadelphia church practiced the Word that they preached and did not deny the name of Jesus Christ.

Stages of Spiritual Growth

I am not trying to minimize the importance of the messages given to the other six churches, for every Christian has or will experience the personality trait of each of these seven churches of Asia Minor. My point is that the Philadelphia church is the best one to use as a role model to find an open door.

I would be a liar if I said that I never left my first love and did not have to do my first works over again like the church at Ephesus.

I would be a fool if I did not acknowledge and respect the tenacity of the church at Smyrna that suffered great persecution and even went to prison for the cause of Christ.

We can all learn from the believers at Pergamos who were faithful in their allegiance to the name of Jesus, but who fell and got involved with false doctrines inspired by the devil.

The church also has a lot to learn from the Christians at Thyatira who allowed a Jezebel to practice evil and ungodly prophets to disgrace their profession of faith. They even permitted fornication to abound in their very midst.

The church at Sardis was a dried-up, stale church whose works were not perfect before God because the majority of them were as spiritually cold as a block of ice.

The Laodicean church was like many believers in today's society who could not take a stand. They were neither hot (on fire for Jesus Christ) or cold (dead spiritually). They were lukewarm. God hated the taste of their worship so much that He spit it out.

Every Christian has visited each of these places in his or her own spiritual development. That's not all bad because each stage represents growth.

If you have lost your first love, the church of Ephesus is a good role model to show you how to get Him back in your life. If fornication and adultery preoccupy your mind, the church of Thyatira might be able to help you and tell you what Jesus told them.

If you want to walk through the doorway of destiny, you have to understand some clearly defined prerequisites. The church of Philadelphia can tell us from experience what they are.

Three Steps to Your Destiny

We must take three crucial, essential steps in order to walk through the doorway of destiny:

1. We must acknowledge that we have little strength.

We are not the source of unlimited power, but God is—and He lives in us.

We must accept and then acknowledge that it is not by our own might or power that we can succeed in life; it is only by the Spirit of the Lord that the road to true success is divinely paved. Then, we must get busy and work on finishing the course.

2. We must keep God's Word.

When you keep something, you cherish it. Some women will keep their first rose folded in a love letter. Some men keep a baseball that was signed by their favorite player.

God desires for us to keep His Word daily. Psalm 119:11 says:

Thy word have I hid in mine heart, that I might not sin against thee.

This Scripture should not be a secret to the church; it is a weapon that we should use every day.

It is fairly easy to get saved. The only thing you have to do is confess with your mouth and believe in your heart that Jesus is the risen Lord. (See Romans 10:9,10.) Your confession is then transformed into salvation.

The hard part is living a holy, sanctified life. That is the reason we need to keep the Word—in order to make it through the door.

In "Destiny of Holiness," a heart-moving meditation in the book *My Utmost For His Highest,* Oswald Chambers writes, "Holiness means unsullied walking with feet, unsullied talking with tongue, unsullied thinking with the mind—every detail of the life under the scrutiny of God. Holiness is not only what God gives me, but what I manifest that God has given me."[6]

3. We must not deny Jesus' name.

On Elvis Presley's birthday his fans won't deny his name. But you can't even compare the king of rock and roll to the Rock of Ages and the Kings of Kings.

Demons tremble at the very mention of the name of Jesus. We must always respect His title for He is the Christ, the Son of the living God.

At the same time, we can have a relationship with the Savior because He had an earthly name and an earthly body and died an earthly death. The name of Jesus represents that He was tempted just like you and me. He was a physical man who felt the pains of life. Jesus could do something about those pains because He was, and still is, Christ the Anointed.

Still, I thank God because I can also relate to Jesus, the carpenter's son, who did ordinary things like you and me. There is power in Jesus' name because Jesus Christ is the best role model alive to show us how to walk through the doorways of destiny.

The Philadelphia church gives us a blueprint on how to discover the essence of destiny, how to walk through the doorway of destiny, how to do the greater works of preaching, teaching, and working miracles, how to live for God in the last days, and how to be ready when Jesus comes.

> **God has a doorway of destiny that He wants each and every one of us to walk through.**

Chapter 9

Destined for Deliverance

"Better keep yourself clean and bright; you are the window through which you must see the world."–George Bernard Shaw

A young lady whom I know got saved, sanctified, and satisfied with Jesus Christ. But she still had one problem that plagued her spiritual life. She cursed constantly like a dirty old sailor. Although she loved the Lord with her whole heart, she was not totally delivered from the habit of vulgar verbiage and gutter talk.

What was the problem? This Christian young lady had not walked through the doorway of destiny in the area of her daily vocabulary.

Although she was extremely active in church, attending Sunday school, morning service, evening service, as well as midweek Bible class, she was still losing the war over her speech. Her vulgarity severely limited her vision and disrupted her destiny because she was disobeying God's Word, which specifically says:

Keep thy tongue from evil, and thy lips from speaking guile. Depart from evil, and do good; seek peace and pursue it. The eyes of the Lord are upon the righteous, and his ears are open unto their cry (Psalm 34:13–15).

One day this Christian young woman decided she would change her destiny. She constantly prayed this prayer:

Set a watch, O Lord, before my mouth; keep the door of my lips (Psalm 141:3).

Then every time she had the desire to curse, she cried out the name of her Savior. When she got upset because someone mistreated her, she called for Jesus. This ultimate five-letter word carried much more weight than her regular four-letter expletives.

As a result, this young lady learned to follow the admonishment of the apostle Paul, who wrote under the anointing of the Holy Spirit:

Be ye angry, and sin not: let not the sun go down upon your wrath: Neither give place to the devil (Ephesians 4:26,27).

God's Back-Up Plan for Single Parents

While God's love is unconditional, the sequence of destiny is conditional.

When a father leaves his family—or remains in the home but is totally irresponsible—destiny is delayed and greatly disturbed. God's perfect will for the interpersonal development of the entire family cannot be fulfilled, and His back-up plan instantly goes into effect.

While the mother and children can reach the mark of excellence on an individual and personal basis, it will be much harder for them to get to that point. In fact, many women and children become victims of their circumstances and never reach their full potential in life.

Single parents, both male and female, who are saved, sanctified, living for God, and teaching their children biblical principles—in spite of their circumstances—are to be commended and encouraged.

Living a kingdom lifestyle in these last days teaches us to treat our families like precious gold and work to provide and protect them. This is the lifestyle that will build the church and win the lost through the power of example.

Single parents who decide to follow Christ, even when their mates forsake the Lord and the family, are to be praised. Wounded single fathers who care for their children, without the support or help of their partner, need a timely, rhema word from the Lord to help them walk through their personally designed, God-ordained doorway of destiny.

Don't give in, my sister and brother. Catch the vision of victory and never give up on your future. By being there for yourself and your children, you are doing the will of God.

It is also the responsibility of the church to become the extended family for single parents. Remember, we serve a God Who is "a father of the fatherless" (Psalm 68:5) and a mother to the motherless.

Guard Your Heart

In the midst of the disappointments of life, we must develop a destiny-driven, inner determination to turn over our turmoil, crisis, and chaos to the creative control and sound advice of Jesus Christ.

Jesus can provide us with the extra power to run our course of destiny with patience while we tread the stress-inducing difficulties of our lives. Stressful scenarios will surely come our way, but if we trust in the Lord Jesus Christ, He will be our partner in productivity concerning how to cope with the hard core issues of life.

Listen closely to the practical words of wisdom found in the book of Proverbs. God uses a key biblical principle to unlock the doorway of destiny that leads us into a new realm of accountability and integrity.

Keep thy heart with all diligence; for out of it are the issues of life (Proverbs 4:23).

The Living Bible puts this verse in plain terms:

Above all else, guard your affections. For they influence everything else in your life.

Why does this verse emphasize that we keep our hearts and guard our affections and desires with diligence? Because the heart—the spirit of man—is the navigating compass, the cruise control that directs the completion of divine destiny. That's the way God designed it. The concrete choices that are made from the heart of humanity, God's creation, dictate whether or not the issues of life will be the force that empowers us or destroys us.

Never before in history has the world been bombarded with so many problems. Every generation has its own incurable disease, but somehow the scientists discovered a lasting cure. Every generation has its own racial, social, and economic problems, but at least there was a clear mandate from the people in support of their leaders who held out a clarion voice of truth.

Adultery, AIDS, teens having babies, cancer, crime, drug abuse, fornication, homosexuality, homelessness, incest, peer pressure, sexual abuse, and rape are just a few of the issues that plague our nation and wound our churches directly and indirectly—whether we want to admit it or not.

That is why we must guard our heart in order to effectively speak and apply God's overcoming Word to these current situations. We cannot ignore the issues of the day, but we must approach them with an outlook based firmly on the Scriptures.

No matter what the issue, the church needs Christians who will stand up and strive for excellence in every area of life.

A Reason for Being

As Christians, we need to be real for the cause of Christ. The church needs to rediscover its reason for being—our *raison d'etre*—by knowing Who Jesus Christ really is. When we truly understand Who Jesus Christ is, we will discover the predestined purpose of the church—which is that we are saved to serve.

We have been called to consistently communicate the challenging and life-changing gospel of Jesus Christ with clarity, credibility, and confidence.

The Lord of hosts needs consecrated, conscientious objectors who don't want to live in the tents of the wicked. The Creator is calling out for brave, bold, and righteously radical warriors for Jesus Christ who are ready to run, walk, or even crawl toward the doorway of destiny and hold high the blood-stained banner of our Lord.

In our perverse society, we, as Christians, are challenged to address many problems. We know that the Lord is our Shepherd, and we shall not want. God is our Provider—our Jehovah-Jireh, the Lord God Who will provide.

Within our communities, however, countless numbers of homeless men and women live on the streets without food or shelter. Within our own families or sphere of influence, we know people who have been affected by AIDS, a disease for which there is no known cure. Certainly God would have us to be concerned about these social problems.

Providing Solutions

What about the drug crisis? It affects our young people and even the adults of the community.

You may ask, "What does that have to do with me?"

Every teenager and adult who is on drugs is one more individual who cannot do the work of the Lord and fulfill his or her destiny. Because they haven't come to their senses, they are still in a quandary and not in control of their destiny or their future.

They may come to church, but God cannot accomplish His complete will in their lives until they admit their need for help. We must face these problems and social conditions.

Teenage pregnancies are often precipitated by children wanting to have children to give themselves a sense of security. With no one to look up to, they have been taught no values on which to base their lives.

The church must have some solutions.

How should we address these social ills that are ripping apart our community? We may say that God will forgive them—and that is true—but we also need to address the issue of destiny. We must make people aware of the fact that God desires for each of us to accomplish certain things in our lives. Unless we get in line with God's will, we risk missing His perfect plan for us.

God has a purpose, a design for each and every one of our lives. Our responsibility is to encourage each person to discover his or her personal divine destiny and walk in it. This includes not only church leadership but members of the congregation. All of us must draw closer to God to find out our particular ministry in life. We have to sell people on the benefits of kingdom living—how they can live more abundantly.

Jesus said:

The thief cometh not, but for to steal, and to kill, and to destroy: I am come that they might have life, and that they might have it more abundantly (John 10:10).

We know that the enemy is at work, but, at the same time, we must provide a clear example of the ministry of the church.

What is the ministry of the church? It is to provide the ministry of reconciliation, as described in 2 Corinthians 5:18,19:

> And all things are of God, who hath reconciled us to himself by Jesus Christ, and hath given to us the ministry of reconciliation; To wit, that God was in Christ, reconciling the world unto himself, not imputing their trespasses unto them; and hath committed unto us the word of reconciliation.

God, through Jesus, came to reconcile the world unto Himself. Now the ministry of reconciliation is accomplished as the Holy Spirit works in God's people—the church—to bring the lost to Christ.

Our job is to bring the lost back to God. Whether the lost is a drug addict, a prostitute, an AIDS patient, a young man who is in jail, a neglectful husband, an unfaithful wife—we have a ministry of reconciliation to bring healing to the situation.

Choosing Between Two Destinies

In the story of the prodigal son, the two sons represent two destinies.

> And he said, A certain man had two sons: And the younger of them said to his father, Father, give me the portion of goods that falleth to me. And he divided unto them his living. And not many days after the younger son gathered all together, and took his journey into a far country, and there wasted his substance with riotous living (Luke 15:11–13).

The younger son said to the father, "You have a great estate and more money than you can count. I want you to give me some of this wealth so I can go out and do my own thing, in my own way, in my own time."

After the father gave the greedy and rebellious son a portion of his wealth, the son went to a distant country and got caught up in wild living and spending money frivolously. He went from bar to bar, looking for a good time and buying his way into popularity.

Before long, he lost sight of his identity. He forgot his sense of purpose and family. His heritage, where he came from, and what his name represented no longer mattered to him. He began to do things that were inconsistent with the training he received in his household.

The Bible says:

Whatsoever a man soweth, that shall he also reap (Galatians 6:7).

You can get away with it for a little while, but the Bible also says:

Be sure your sin will find you out (Numbers 32:23).

You can joke around and say, "Hey, I'm gonna sin, but then I can pray and ask the Lord to forgive me."

Before long, God will blow your cover and reveal the truth about your sinful life. In recent years, God exposed sin in the lives of some of America's most visible evangelists. Don't think for a moment that He will spare you. God's Word will be fulfilled.

From the Mansion to a Mess

The prodigal son's luck soon ran out. A great famine occurred in the land, leaving few resources. During famine, rain doesn't fall, and the rivers dry up. The reservoirs become empty. In the time of famine, people are desperate to get some nourishment. Famine is no respecter of persons, and everyone becomes poor.

And when he had spent all, there arose a mighty famine in that land; and he began to be in want. And he went and joined himself to a citizen of that country; and he sent him into his fields to feed swine. And he would fain have filled his belly with the husks that the swine did eat: and no man gave unto him (Luke 15:14–16).

This young man had depleted his resources, wasting it on wild living and pleasure. He had gone from living in a mansion to living in the mud and muck with the pigs. A resident of that country had given him the lowly job of working in the pigpen.

His existence was so bad that he desired to eat the slop that the pigs ate.

Pigs are swine who will eat anything. That is why when Jesus cast the legion of demons out of a man, they immediately went into the pigs. Pigs wallow in the mud and are not particular about anything. They are just plain messy. That is how low this young man had sunk. He was beginning to think and act like a pig. He had virtually given up.

This scenario provides the classic example of someone going from riches to rags, from the mansion to a mess.

Coming to Your Senses

Finally, as he was wallowing in despair, the young man came to his senses and thought, "Right now, back at home, my father has servants who will give me anything I want to eat."

And when he came to himself, he said, How many hired servants of my father's have bread enough and to spare, and I perish with hunger! I will arise and go to my father, and will say unto him, Father, I have sinned against heaven, and before thee, and am no more worthy to be called thy son: make me as one of thy hired servants (Luke 15:17–19).

Remember, no matter what problems you're going through, the first thing God requires is for you to come to your senses. When you run away from the Father in an effort to do your own thing, you are out of God's perfect will. The farther you go, the harder it is to pull yourself out.

This young man realized he did not have the inner fortitude—not by his own might, nor by his power—to change his depraved condition. Only the Spirit of the Lord could enable him to come to his senses and decide to turn his life around.

To make a decision is the most powerful thing you will ever do. The Bible says:

Choose you this day whom ye will serve (Joshua 24:15).

You and I are going to have to answer for the choices we make because our choices control our future and our destiny.

This young man made a decision and began the journey to his father's home. Along the way, he must have been thinking, "What's going to happen when I get home? Will my father reject me? Will he cast me aside?"

Many times a mother will be more understanding and sympathetic, but the father will say, "Hey, you better get your act together or don't come back into my house." In this case, however, the father responded differently. When he saw his son coming down the road, he had compassion on him.

And he arose, and came to his father. But when he was yet a great way off, his father saw him, and had compassion, and ran, and fell on his neck, and kissed him. And the son said unto him, Father, I have sinned against heaven, and in thy sight, and am no more worthy to be called thy son. But the Father said to his servants, Bring forth the best robe, and put it on him; and put a ring on his hand, and shoes on his feet: And bring hither the fatted calf, and kill it; and let us eat, and be merry: For this my son was dead, and is alive again; he was lost, and is found. And they began to be merry (Luke 15:20–23).

As the son came down this long and winding road, with his head drooping in despair, all he could do was hope for restoration and to be taken back into the family. When his father saw him coming, he ran out and threw his arms of love and protection around him. Immediately, he let his son know that he was going to bring him back into the fold.

The father told his servants to bring the best robe, a ring for his finger, and shoes for his feet. Why? "For my son, who was once dead, is now alive. The one who was lost has come home."

Once we have come to our senses, we must come home to God in order to walk through our personal doorway of destiny. Oswald Chambers stated, "Jesus Christ will not help me obey Him, I must obey Him; and when I obey Him, I fulfill my spiritual destiny."[7]

The Homecoming

When we return home, however, we must also realize that there may be jealousy—even in the church; but we must go on anyhow.

Now his elder son was in the field: and as he came and drew nigh to the house, he heard musick and dancing. And he called one of the servants, and asked what these things meant. And he said unto him, Thy brother is come; and thy father hath killed the fatted calf, because he hath received him safe and sound.

And he was angry, and would not go in: therefore came his father out, and intreated him. And he answering said to his father, Lo, these many years do I serve thee, neither transgressed I at any time thy commandment: and yet thou never gavest me a kid, that I might make merry with my friends: But as soon as this thy son was come, which hath devoured thy living with harlots, thou hast killed for him the fatted calf.

And he said unto him, Son, thou art ever with me, and all that I have is thine. It was meet [fitting] that we should make merry, and be glad: for this thy brother was dead, and is alive again; and was lost, and is found (Luke 15:25–32).

The prodigal son's older brother became jealous. He told his father, "I was here all the time. I didn't sin. I served you faithfully, and now you embrace this outcast. You bring out the fatted calf for my brother who has wasted your money on prostitutes, and you push me aside. You've forgotten about me."

Listen to the words of wisdom from the father who said, "Son, you are always with me. Instead of being jealous, you need to thank God that you are in the ark of safety. Thank God that you're saved and living for Jesus. Thank God that you're not out on the streets and that you're not dead."

We must have understanding and compassion toward those who are lost. Jesus came to save those who are lost—not those who are already saved!

When that young man was out there doing the wild thing, partying and dancing, he thought it would go on forever, but the money ran out.

You can live in sin and you can lie, but "be sure your sin will find you out" (Numbers 32:23). Don't play with destiny. Don't play with God's preordained plan. You've spent enough time in sin and hypocrisy.

Before it's too late, it's time for you to come home to the Father and walk through your personal doorway of destiny.

Before long, God will blow your cover and reveal the truth about your sinful life.

Chapter 10

Is Destiny I.Q.?

"Nothing in the world can take the place of persistence. Talent will not. Nothing is more common than unsuccessful men with talent. Genius will not. Unrewarded genius is almost a proverb. Education will not. The world is full of educated derelicts. Persistence, determination, and hard work make the difference."–President Calvin Coolidge

Destiny is the God–given source of motivation, the predetermined plan that compels us to succeed through the storms and struggles of life–even when we were not supposed to make it according to the standards of man.

William W. Brown, a former slave and the first African American to write a novel, said, "Destiny lies not in the stars, but in our hearts."

To measure intelligence, an I.Q. (intelligence quotient) test is given to students. I.Q., however, is not synonymous with destiny because it does not take into account the final results of these tests.

Destiny, on the other hand, considers every single component that the Creator has included as part of our lives even before time began. (See Ephesians 1:3–5.)

One of these components is educational excellence, which is of utmost importance in the kingdom of God. As 2 Timothy 2:15 declares:

> Study to shew thyself approved unto God, a workman that needeth not to be ashamed, rightly dividing the word of truth.

The Bell Curve Myth

A recent *New York Times* best-selling book titled, *The Bell Curve*, left many analysts asking the question, "Is I.Q. equivalent to destiny?"

In the October 24, 1994 edition of *Newsweek*, Tom Morganthau writes that Murray and Hernstein, *The Bell Curve* authors, say the evidence of a black-white I.Q. gap is overwhelming.

They think the difference helps explain why many blacks seemed destined to remain mired in poverty, and they insist that whites and blacks alike must face up to the reality of black intellectual disadvantage. Nevertheless, they maintain that the differences should have no bearing on the way individual whites and blacks view each other.

The Bell Curve strongly suggests that African Americans on average score 15 points lower on I.Q. tests than whites, and whites score lower than Asians, according to its data. The conclusion, therefore, is that poor people who have lower I.Q.s are doomed to a destiny of damnation. The authors recommend that all the government funded programs targeted toward the poor must cease since it is a losing battle.

In response to *The Bell Curve* theory, Les Payne wrote in the *Newsday* column, dated November 20, 1994, that "the notion of black inferiority, as espoused by Murray/Hernstein and Shockley/Jensen before them, and Hitler in *Mein Kampf* ahead of them, is once again an acceptable subject of debate."

Mr. Payne further stated:

This positive-sounding, though nonetheless bogus theory would likely break up in heavy weather. Yet, working the disadvantaged side of Nazi nonsense is almost what Murray/Hernstein have done in their attempts to prove black intellectual capacity inferior as a genetic given. Measured I.Q. in this former slave republic, Murray/Hernstein shamelessly argue—as if all else were equal—is what determines . . . one's achievement in society.

The authors of *The Bell Curve,* Harvard psychologists Richard J. Hernstein and Charles Murray, never take into account the influence of slavery and the lasting death blows of a widespread slave mentality embedded in the minds of many African Americans. They fail to realize that this slavery mentality can only be overcome through spiritual motivation and decisive action.

I wholeheartedly agree with Grambling University Coach, Eddie Robinson, who said, "The will to win, the desire to succeed, the urge to reach your full potential . . . these are the keys that will unlock the door to personal excellence."

Destiny's Bottom Line

The argument presented in *The Bell Curve* has been in the making for a long time, and its research and data is financially backed by a major foundation.

Mr. Payne said, "This best-selling book by Charles Murray and Richard Hernstein grants the dominant society a blanket innocence to all economic acts of racism short of direct murder."

When examples of African Americans with high I.Q.s are mentioned, however, it is called the exception and not the norm. This is the type of verbal hype and foolish propaganda that was circulated before Hitler exterminated the Jews during the Holocaust.

The message contained within the 850 pages of *The Bell Curve* is in direct opposition to the message of Jesus Christ who preached:

The Spirit of the Lord is upon me, because he hath anointed me to preach the gospel to the poor; he hath sent me to heal the brokenhearted, to preach deliverance to the captives, and recovering of sight to the blind, to set at liberty them that are bruised. To preach the acceptable year of the Lord (Luke 4:18,19).

This is the gospel Jesus Christ preached. This is the motivational gospel that leads to repentance, transformation, and reformation.

The Bell Curve strongly implies that the time to heal the broken-hearted has come and now is long gone. The major dilemma that rocks the soul and very conscious of our nation is that Christians are buying into this selfish philosophy of me, myself, and my splendid I.Q.

Whether we belong to the Christian Coalition or the Rainbow Coalition, as Christians, we must raise questions about an I.Q. test that is designed for certain segments of the population and then given to everyone at random.

The bottom line is that destiny is not determined by I.Q. How do we know? Because Proverbs 1:7 declares:

The fear of the Lord is the beginning of knowledge: but fools despise wisdom and instruction.

Jesus Christ is the "author and finisher of our faith" (Hebrews 12:2)—and our destiny. Whatever you think you are lacking, God has already placed in you to fulfill your life's work, your personal destiny.

Reaching Your Mind's Potential

Genesis 1:26 declares:

And God said, Let us make man in our image, after our likeness.

All of humanity—red, yellow, black, and white—are made in the image of God. God is an intelligent being Who brought light where there was once darkness. Human beings are intelligent because we are made in the image of God.

The noted French philosopher, Renee Descartes, stated, "I think, therefore I am." Long before Descartes, however, the writer of Proverbs had declared God's truth concerning man.

For as he thinketh in his heart, so is he (23:7a).

The fact is this: You can change your destiny. It doesn't matter whether you finished grade school, high school, or college. Even a person who is a complete failure in the eyes of society can be transformed through the power of God, as Romans 12:1,2 declares:

I beseech you therefore, brethren, by the mercies of God, that ye present your bodies a living sacrifice, holy, acceptable unto God, which is your reasonable service. And be not conformed to this world: but be ye transformed by the renewing of your mind, that ye may prove what is that good, and acceptable, and perfect, will of God.

Being transformed by the renewing of the mind is the key to fulfilling the perfect will of God. People can be transformed if they get the right information to change their lives. With God, no situation is hopeless.

The children of God possess a superior form of intelligence that is far greater than I.Q. God's Word makes this clear:

For who hath known the mind of the Lord, that he may instruct him? But we have the mind of Christ (1 Corinthians 2:16).

The apostle Paul clarifies this bold statement more plainly in Philippians 2:5, which states:

Let this mind be in you, which was also in Christ Jesus.

When Jesus Christ talked about His preaching ministry, He told the world what was on His mind. He was concerned about preaching to the poor, healing the brokenhearted, preaching deliverance to the captives, recovering of sight to the blind, and setting free those who are bruised; that's what Jesus Christ thought, spoke about publicly, and practiced daily.

We need that same frame of mind, the mind of Christ. We need to not accept the philosophy of *The Bell Curve*. As the church, we must cast down these vain imaginations and high sounding philosophies of man that exalt themselves against the knowledge of God.

$50 Hairdos and Five-Cent Brains

If given the opportunity and placed in a nurturing environment, African Americans can excel just like anyone else.

I have personally seen a homeless single parent find an apartment and get her kids into school. Today those same children are excelling in their education because that single parent and other strong, positive, extended family role models cared enough to encourage them.

Being middle class or filthy rich is not the answer to the problems that plague our society. If an individual does not change his line of thinking and practice concrete principles of success, the fruit of his labor will always be failure—regardless of race.

Plenty of people have $50 hairdos and five-cent brains, only because they—and the people they choose as role models—have no desire to increase their knowledge or develop their minds.

On the other hand, there are countless examples of strong African Americans who have succeeded in our culture. Great black men like John H. Johnson, the publisher of *Ebony* magazine, and Earl

Graves, the publisher of *Black Enterprise.* Oprah Winfrey, the famed talk show host; Susan Taylor, noted author and editor of *Essence* magazine; and Maya Angelou, the renowned poet and writer, are excellent examples of intelligent black women succeeding in their chosen fields.

Dr. Charles Drew, who performed the first blood transfusion, and died when he was in need of one; psychologist, Dr. Alvin Pousaint of Harvard Medical School, whose work has touched the lives of millions; and the noted brain surgeon, Dr. Ben Carson, are all living proof that I.Q. is important. Their destiny, however, was developed in the hands of God Who taught them discipline through ordinary, down-to-earth role models—people who cared for them and helped them reach their potential.

Facts Versus Truth

The Bell Curve, based upon the supposed factual data compiled by the late Richard J. Hernstein and Charles Murray, suggests that African Americans are inferior as a whole in spite of the truth that many successful African Americans are excelling greatly within our culture.

Dr. Alvin Pousaint of Harvard Medical School stated in *Newsweek,* "They're saying it's science, but it has a racist effect." He further notes that for "whites who are already predisposed to believe that blacks are inferior, this is going to confirm their prejudices."

The authors of *The Bell Curve* did not take into consideration this one truth: Facts are subject to change, but biblical principles are eternal. Also, the facts of the day are not always synonymous to the eternal truth.

Slavery was a fact, but it was subject to change. At one time people believed the world was flat, but that fact was subject to change because it was wrong. It was not built on the firm foundation of eternal truth but on the sinking sand of assumption. An assumed fact can be proven wrong, but the eternal truth is irrefutable.

Whenever someone substitutes assumed facts for the eternal truth, their argument is detrimental to society at large.

I imagine that Medgar Evers, Malcolm X, and Martin Luther King, Jr–the three Ms of the civil rights movement–are probably crying out from their graves right now, asking: "Why is the church being silent about this hideous propaganda of race polarization that is politically motivated and certainly not scripturally inspired?"

The life of every African American who succeeds in life–on whatever level–is the strongest argument against *The Bell Curve* and proof that God's Word is true.

African Americans, or any people who are poor, must not accept *The Bell Curve* benediction to inferiority as their manifest destiny. The scientific data within the many pages of *The Bell Curve* is extremely biased and intentionally plays upon the fear of black crime and a deteriorating society.

The truth of the matter is that whites are killing whites, Hispanics are killing Hispanics, blacks are killing blacks, and worst of all, children are murdering children in a new shock wave of domestic violence.

Street gangs are not only found in South Central Los Angeles and New York City but also in rural white communities throughout the nation. The problem of violence in American society goes much deeper than race.

We must not minimize the proliferation of crime in our communities. We must address the problems of the day with concrete principles that lead to success and fulfill destiny.

Superior Intelligence

Rolanda Watts, internationally syndicated talk show host, recently said, "You have to take control of your destiny, and if your destiny is full of negativity, then the first thing you have to do is sweep up your house."

The only answer to racism and negative thinking is a motivating wave of spiritual revival realized through true repentance of the sins of the past and present. That is the only way we can prepare a better foundation for the children who are the future.

Our churches must become training centers, spiritual boot camps, and God-fearing army barracks where young people and adults are trained through motivational messages concerning the Master of their destiny and His plans and purposes for their lives.

Each Monday night at Mt. Sinai Baptist Church, we have our Young Men's and Young Women's Fellowship to teach our young people that they are not inferior, but that they are wonderfully and marvelously made in the image of God, Who is the Epitome of all superior intelligence.

Even if some of us don't receive the same opportunities as the more affluent members of our culture, we tell them, "That doesn't matter," and remind them that Jesus Christ said:

Behold, I have set before thee an open door, and no man can shut it (Revelation 3:8).

The authors of *The Bell Curve* may expect us to accept inferiority as destiny and, using their conclusions, place an entire race of people back in the dark ages of separatism. Others may point out facts about black-on-black crime but ignore principles that change hard-core prisoners into effective gospel preachers who are having a positive impact on their communities.

Facts are subject to change, but it is an eternal principle that if God opens a door for you, no one can shut it–except God or you.

The truth is that I.Q. is not destiny. Destiny is the predetermined plan of the Creator that He gives to each person to actualize, accomplish, and fulfill.

I.Q. cannot be compared to the wisdom of God and the mind of Christ that true bloodwashed believers in Jesus Christ possess. The wisdom of God and the mind of Christ will open doors of new opportunity in spite of the facts, despite the statistics, and no matter what the hype of the hour.

It is best to build our hopes on things eternal and hold onto God's unchanging hands. The wisdom of God is eternal; I.Q. is not.

When I.Q. Doesn't Count

We are all aware of the social problems in America that are the result of moral decay. We know the facts, but what principles can change failures into real life success stories?

We must preach daily through our lifestyles, using the principles of destiny concerning how to succeed in life, step by step, day by day, month by month, year by year, and decade by decade–until Jesus comes and opens the doorway of destiny in heaven. We don't have time to sit in our pews and do nothing but wait until Jesus returns. We, the church, must teach and take action now. We must occupy until Jesus Christ comes again.

We must keep our hearts "with all diligence; for out of it are the issues of life" (Proverbs 4:23).

This verse does not say to keep your I.Q. with all diligence for out of it proceeds the issues of life. The issues of life are determined by the status of the heart–and not I.Q. While I.Q. is extremely important, it is not destiny. Jesus said:

For where your treasure is, there will your heart be also (Matthew 6:21).

People find themselves in all kinds of trouble and in all types of compromising binds because the desires of their hearts have been misdirected by the influence of peer pressure and low self-esteem. If your heart is in the area of crime and violence, your treasure is there and not in heaven.

It is not a matter of I.Q.; it is a matter of the spiritual condition of your heart and the renewal of your mind with positive information concerning who God says you are.

The world may say you are a worthless idiot, but God says you are more than a conqueror through Christ Jesus. The world may say you will never amount to anything, but God says that you can do all things through Christ who strengthens you. The world may say you never should have been born, you're just a waste of time and energy, you're a worthless piece of trash, but God says that before you were in your mother's womb I ordained you, I sanctified you, and called you a prophet unto the nations.

What God says about you is eternal truth that you can always depend on.

Think God Thoughts

Whether you have a high I.Q. of 165, or a dull I.Q. of 76, think God thoughts, think power thoughts because your mind can be programmed for success.

As he thinketh in his heart, so is he (Proverbs 23:7).

Matthew 19:26 says:

But with God all things are possible.

The apostle Paul, through the inspiration of the Holy Spirit, tells us how to develop our thought pattern for effectiveness and excellence in life:

Finally, brethren, whatsoever things are true, whatsoever things are honest, whatsoever things are just, whatsoever things are pure, whatsoever things are lovely, whatsoever things are of good report; if there be any virtue, and if there be any praise, think on these things (Philippians 4:8).

The fact that plenty of African Americans have high I.Q.s refutes the argument that African Americans are inferior in the area of intelligence.

I.Q. is not developed on the basis of whether you are rich or poor, but, more importantly, on the basis of someone spending quality time with a child—reading to him, loving him, being his mentor and his hero. It is a matter of letting that child know early, between the ages of one and four, that he is wonderfully and marvelously made in the image of God—and God don't make no junk.

A recent *Ebony* magazine article, titled "How To Program Your Child For Success" by Muriel L. Whetstone, stated:

The first task, they say, is to love your child and to surround him or her with a challenging environment that stimulates curiosity. The second task, flowing with and out of the first, is to select a good school and to participate actively in his or her school life. The third task, which is usually neglected . . . is to take advantage of the events sponsored by museums, libraries, and other educational institutions that can be found in almost every community. . . . Providing children with experiences related to their expressed curiosities helps expand their thinking.

My goal isn't to minimize the impact of I.Q.; it is to maximize the true influence of destiny. Since I.Q. is not destiny, a strong sense of destiny allows ordinary people, whom the experts predicted to fail, to excel beyond their highest expectations.

More Than a Second Chance

Destiny is much more than a second chance; it is God's original plan for our personal success.

So don't look down on the poor through your lofty spectacles and say, "You're worthless because you don't have a high I.Q. and an Ivy League degree like me." How selfish and self-serving can you be?

William Julius Wilson, writing in the *New York Times,* made this observation:

> Take a white or black middle-class family and strip them of all their resources to make them comparable to an inner-city family. Put them in one of those dangerous neighborhoods where the parents have to worry every day about what's going to happen to their children. Where they have to deal with the crime, the drugs, and isolation. Where they can't depend on other families in the neighborhood because they're also isolated. You put any family in that neighborhood, stick them there, let them be trapped, and see how successful they'll be over the long run in raising their children.

At one time in history, the experts called our Japanese brothers and sisters inferior, but time proved that argument totally erroneous. The answer to society's present ills is not to tell the spiritually hungry youth and the masses of poor people that they are destined for failure. It would be far more productive to tell them the eternal truth—that we have an inheritance and we were:

> Predestinated according to the purpose of him who worketh all things after the counsel of his own will (Ephesians 1:11).

Walking through the doorway of destiny is a matter of caring enough to teach ordinary people—regardless of race— how to succeed in spite of their condition of existence. If you want to help somebody, teach them what true destiny is —God's perfect plan for their personal success.

Let your hair down and reach out to them on their level. It takes a city, a community, and even a church to save a child's future and destiny.

> ## *The wisdom of God is eternal; I.Q. is not.*

Chapter 11

Your Motivational Guide

"The journey of a thousand miles starts with a single step."
– Chinese proverb

The problems of this present age are not the result of low I.Q. Most of society's ills are the direct result of an entire generation that has grown up with no father.

In addition to the fatherless household, our political leadership represents—in too many cases—irresponsible father figures, called politicians, who care only about themselves. Even the majority of our churches lack the discipline, training, and, more importantly, the presence of fathers.

Society has waged a major war against fathers, thereby destroying the nuclear structure of the family. The father represents the head of the household. Without a father, there is no vision.

Where there is no vision, the people perish (Proverbs 29:18).

God, however, has raised up single parents who become both mother and father to their children. Without their dedication, our society would be in complete anarchy.

Satan wants to destroy men and fathers and their manhood in order to ruin the family that God created, organized, and authorized. Satan has strategically set up road blocks to hinder God's men from walking through the necessary spiritual developmental stages— life's doorways of destiny. The devil hates when a man worships God and discovers his personal destiny to be a leader.

As an African-American man, I vividly see how satan is destroying the lives of millions of black men. Whether it is O. J. Simpson, Michael Jackson, Tupac Shakur, Daryl Strawberry, or Mike Tyson, satan is out to destroy black men because of their potential to be outstanding men of destiny who can help others.

Satan's tactics, however, do not negate the black man's, or anyone else's, personal responsibility to resist the devil. That old Flip Wilson excuse, "the devil made me do it," will not work.

The devil can only attack and tempt. You are the one who either decides to give in to the forces of evil or resist the devil.

An Endangered Species?

At no other time since the days of slavery and the civil rights movement have the forces of evil, satan himself, come against the black male with such voracity as in 1994. It was a year full of court cases and legal accusations against black males. This attack of the enemy is not only focused on African-American males, but they are disproportionately targeted by demonic forces more than any other group.

African-American males are the major targets of drugs and alcohol abuse and crime. Sure, these things happen in other communities also, but they dominate the black community. Why? Not because of low I.Q. scores but because of the absence of fathers in the black community.

A *New York Times* magazine article dated December 4, 1994, carried the title, "The Black Man Is In Terrible Trouble. Whose Problem Is It? A Round–Table Discussion Between Patrick Day, Ken Hamblin, Joseph Marshal, Hugh Price, John Singleton and William Julius Wilson, Moderated by Bob Herbert." The article made this statement:

> In America, the leading cause of death among black males between the ages of 15 and 24 is homicide. The unemployment rate in America for black males is more than twice that of white males. Even black men with jobs and higher education do not, for the most part, receive the same pay as white men or black women.

It is not I.Q. that hinders the black man from fulfilling his destiny. The real perpetrator is a lack of jobs and subtle, as well as overt, racism in the workplace that fails to appreciate the worth of the black male.

To make matters worse, employers pit the black male against the black woman by making her a double minority. We are in this together—male and female, black and white—for whatever hits the black community first is eventually going to affect every other community in some way.

Who is Jesus?

Why does satan come against black men with such force? I believe it is the same reason he comes against our Jewish brothers and sisters.

Satan, once an archangel in heaven in charge of worship, was previously named Lucifer. You can bet that satan vividly remembers what Jesus, Who was a Jew, looked like when He walked this earth.

The December 1994 issue of *Life* magazine included an interesting feature article titled, "Solving the Mystery of Jesus and Why It Matters Today. Who Was He?"

The Bible pulls no punches concerning Who Jesus is. He is the Son of God. He is the Savior of all human kind. According to the book of Revelation, however, this godly Semitic man did not look anything like Michaelangelo's painting of Jesus.

The book of Revelation describes the texture of His hair, the look in His eyes, the tone of His voice, and the color of His skin:

His head and his hairs were white like wool, as white as snow; and his eyes were as a flame of fire; And his feet like unto fine brass, as if they burned in a furnace; and his voice as the sound of many waters (Revelation 1:14,15).

Today we would describe Jesus as having a head full of white hair. The references to "like wool" and "white as snow" refer to Jesus' hair and not His face. Black people have hair with a wool-like texture.

Although Scripture does not describe the features of Jesus' face—which I believe God purposely omitted to avoid racism within the church—it does tell us the color of His skin. His feet were "like unto fine brass, as if they burned in a furnace." Sounds like a golden charcoal color to me.

What about His voice? I believe it had the deep intonation and resonance of a Paul Robeson, James Earl Jones, or Ozzie Davis. Jesus spoke with authority and with a voice of eternal truth, with a voice like that of Rev. Dr. Martin Luther King, Jr. or William Seymour. Jesus had a preacher's voice that roared like Niagara Falls.

The Ultimate Argument Against Racism

Based on these eternal truths, one can understand why satan is intimidated by the black man and wants to pit him against the Jewish man—because we have a common link in Jesus Christ.

This is not a racist argument. The genealogy of Jesus Christ proves that every single race of people upon the entire face of the earth can be found in the bloodline of Jesus Christ.

The descendants of Noah–Shem, Ham, and Japheth–were used by God to populate the earth after the flood. The Jewish race came from Shem's descendants; Ham's descendants developed into the black race; and Japheth was the father of the white face.

Amazingly, all three races are represented in the lineage of Jesus Christ, making the Son of God a mixture of all the races that descended from Noah's sons. God, in His infinite wisdom, knew that the Savior of the world must have the blood of all races flowing in His veins.

Jesus' interracial makeup makes Him the ultimate argument against racism. In other words, it is impossible to call yourself a Christian and be a racist of any kind. Jesus said:

> And the King shall answer and say unto them, Verily I say unto you, Inasmuch as ye have done it unto one of the least of these my brethren, ye have done it unto me (Matthew 25:40).

The way we treat others reflects the way we would treat Jesus if He walked the earth today.

When we understand Who Jesus is, the door of our minds opens to embrace all people collectively. Since the true church, the body of Christ, is made up of people of all races throughout the world, we must begin to worship together and work alongside one another to bring glory to our universal Savior Who died to save us all.

Racial Reconciliation

The brutal reality of racial hatred is spreading through America like wild fire. The horrible burning of more than 30 historic southern black churches in the past 18 months, and the torching of racially mixed churches that don't espouse the rhetoric of the Klu Klux Klan, should drive the entire church to her knees in prayer.

Many of these once beautiful works of southern architecture were over 100 years old. Poor, southern black folk put their hard-earned, money together for decades to build a place where they could worship God in spirit and in truth. I believe this vicious, racist act against God's people could, ironically, be the exact force that drives the church to a true revival that the arsonists will regret forever.

What satan designed for evil, God will work for our good. In response to these hate crimes, the true church—made up of the redeemed from every race in our nation—will hit the streets and show the world what it means to follow Jesus Christ.

Not everyone in the church will see it that way. For many people, these horrible acts of racism will only further the divide between blacks and whites. Those who are sensitive to the move of the Holy Spirit, however, will realize that it is time to come together. The move of God will begin to spread like wild fire outside the church, in the streets, on the corner, in the parks, on beaches, and even before the seat of government.

Now is the time to speak out publicly and privately against all forms of racism. We must begin to boldly preach the message of racial reconciliation. God can save a sin-sick Klu Klux Klan man. God can save a skin head. God can save a Nazi. God can even save a black separatist. Jesus saves to the uttermost.

The church is neither black nor white. When a predominantly black church is torched, it is a sin against God Himself and an act of injustice against His entire church. Why? Because God has only one church, one body with many parts. Satan wants to use racial hatred and violence to destroy our communities and inner cities.

Why has he targeted southern black churches for destruction? Because ethnic congregations will play an important role in this coming revival. Black men who are a constant target of satanic attack throughout the nation can find inner healing and hope in many black churches that preach the gospel with power.

Satan is still angered by William Seymour's role in the Azusa Street revival. He is still angered by Rev. Dr. Martin Luther King, Jr.'s role in the civil rights movement. He is angered at the role that black ministers have in this current move of God.

As people of God, we must report these hate crimes immediately. If you see a suspicious individual or group near a church, regardless of the congregation's racial make-up, report it to the police. Don't just sit there and pray. Report it, and then continue to pray in the Spirit. Many black and white Christians may be aware of people in their community who have espoused racial rhetoric and hatred. If you know that they may be responsible for a church fire, report them. It is the right thing to do.

Jesus Christ is the Banner of Truth under which all of us must march. The church must stand against racial hatred in all its forms. Regardless of the color of the perpetrator, we must oppose southern black church burnings, modern job discrimination, real estate red-lining, cross burnings, grafitti defacing a black church or a Jewish synagogue, and rape or murder. God wants the church to abolish every single double-standard, which is the breeding ground for all racial hatred.

If we want to fulfill our divine destiny as Christians from various ethnic backgrounds, if we really want to walk through the door-ways of destiny and fulfill our mission in life, then we must take a stand against all forms of racism.

Give Us Men!

When Jesus shed His blood on Calvary's rugged cross, He truly opened up the doors of equal opportunity for everyone. Dr. Martin Luther King, Jr. was right on target when he said, "Our destinies are tied together; none of us can make it alone."

Jesus Christ is multi-ethnic. Jesus Christ is a man of color. Jesus Christ is a man of struggle, purpose, and destiny.

When I preach, I preach only Jesus Christ Who lived, died, and rose from the dead on the third day. Why? Because the power of the gospel is in the shedding of His blood and the resurrection. That is good news.

In order for our society to come out of the red, we must begin to mix together, worship together, pray together, and even begin to walk through the doorways of destiny together. There is only one way for men and fathers to successfully come out of the red spiritually, economically, and socially, and into the black to save our families. They must reach out to other men who have been through these specific doorways of destiny that those who are struggling desire to walk through.

We need fathers. We need men to take their rightful place in their homes and communities.

The prolific poet, J. G. Holland, said it like this:

God, give us men!
A time like this demands strong minds, great hearts, true faith, and ready hands;
Men whom the lust of office does not kill;
Men whom the spoils of office cannot buy;
Men who possess opinions and a will;
Men who have honor;
Men who will not lie;
Men who can stand before a demagogue and damn his treacherous flatteries without winking;
Tall men, sun-crowned.
Who live above the fog in public duty and in private thinking.

Iron Sharpening Iron

The Bible sets the example for men's ministry and provides a very simple concept that works: older men who dream dreams relate to younger men who see visions (Joel 2:28). Black and white men find inner healing for the sins of the past and the challenges of the present.

Fulfilling the daily plans of the Creator is the most important role any man can have in life. This ministry is a profound doorway of destiny called "the iron sharpeneth iron" men's outreach ministry.

This is the only outreach ministry for men to find inner healing and essential wholeness. Scripture says:

Iron sharpeneth iron; so a man sharpeneth the countenance of his friend (Proverbs 27:17).

This verse does not say "as iron sharpeneth bricks," or "as iron sharpeneth wood." Why? Because some pressures and problems in life can only be understood and shared by another man, or father, who has been through a similar situation and who can relate to his pain.

We must still communicate with our wives because communication is the foundation of success in any relationship. Communication is the compass that leads to destiny. However, there are times in every man's life that we desperately need to open up and share our pain, our hurts, our frustrations, our faults, and our disasters with a *brother* in Christ.

The very appearance, the very countenance of a man is enhanced through this much-ignored doorway of destiny–"the iron sharpeneth iron" men's outreach ministry.

If you are a women reading this book, you can encourage your husband, your brother, your friend, or your pastor to discover the wealth of this type of ministry. If you are a man, begin to open up and find some strong brothers in Christ with whom you can share on a regular basis.

Men of destiny will sharpen one another.

Whatever You Do

Our very existence is totally dependent upon God. Without God we are nothing. Without God there is no hope. Without God there is no future. Without God there is no success. Without Him there is no sense of destiny. Why? Because God is our destiny. It is in God that we have our very existence.

> For in him we live, and move, and have our being; as certain also of your own poets have said, For we are also his offspring (Acts 17:28).

This world is not our home; we are just passing through. We are strangers and sojourners in a foreign land.

In order to truly excel in this temporary journey called life, we must learn to live, move, and find our ultimate pleasure in Christ.

Whatever you do, do it as unto the Lord. If you are an artist, create artwork that is pleasing to the Lord. If you are a writer, write your letters, messages, and music in a way that honors the Lord. If you are a parent, raise your children to fear the Lord. If you are a pastor, lead the flock of God to praise and worship the Lord. If you are a rapper, rap as unto the Lord.

If you are a news reporter, report as unto the Lord. If you are a sanitation worker, do your job as unto the Lord. If you are a social worker, help others in the name of the Lord. If you are a businessman, conduct your business as unto the Lord.

If you are a Christian, live your life for the Lord. If you are a preacher, preach with the Lord's anointing until broken, bruised, and battered lives are changed.

Do everything as unto the Lord. That is how you will learn to walk through life's developmental stages with true victory. That is how you will learn to walk step by step through the divinely appointed doorways of destiny.

Relationships become richer when they are developed as unto the Lord. Work becomes more meaningful when you do it as unto the Lord. Play becomes more pleasurable when you do it as unto the Lord.

When all the demons of hell rise against you, keep living as unto the Lord. When you are pressed against the wall, let God motivate you to move in the right direction.

Your Motivational Guide for Living

In order to fulfill our God-ordained destiny in life, there are several doors you must first walk through:

1. Humility - God wants to motivate you to greatness through the doorway of humility.

Humble yourself therefore under the mighty hand of God, that he may exalt you in due1time (1 Peter 5:6).

Many times, however, we try to exalt ourselves instead of letting the Lord promote His predestined purpose for our ordinary lives.

2. Learning - God wants to motivate us to leadership through the doorway of education, study, and learning.

Study to shew thyself approved unto God, a workman that needeth not to be ashamed, rightly dividing the word of truth (2 Timothy 2:15).

3. Praise and worship - God wants to motivate us to leave our stale religion by walking through the doorway of praise and worship.

Enter into his gates with thanksgiving, and into his courts with praise: be thankful unto him, and bless his name (Psalm 100:4).

These three simple steps can make the difference between fulfilling your destiny and falling flat on your face. There is only one hitch. You can't be humble, understand God's Word, or praise God without the help of the Holy Spirit.

As Christians, we have our own, personal motivational guide living within us—the Holy Spirit.

What can He do for you? The Holy Spirit will:

1. Lead you into all truth.

2. Bring to your remembrance whatever the Lord has taught you in your devotional time with Him.

3. Move you toward the center of God's will.

4. Help you discover the many doors of divine opportunity that Jesus Christ opens for you in your lifetime.

With the Holy Spirit as your motivational Guide, you won't need to work yourself into a frenzy in order to be motivated. The Holy Spirit is a gentle guide Who leads and does not push us through our doorways of destiny.

Ordinary People

I have a good friend who has a deadly form of cancer. His doctors told him that most people with this disease normally don't survive for more than three months after being diagnosed. Yet my friend is still alive after two years.

He changed his diet and receives monthly chemotherapy treatments, but, most of all, he believes that God has opened the door of healing in his life. Through the tears, heartache, and pain, he still believes that Jesus Christ is the Healer and Master of his destiny. Along the way, my friend has matured spiritually in his faith journey, and his daily walk with God has become a passionate love affair with the Creator.

Although the doctors cannot predict the outcome, my friend still walks by faith in spite of the circumstances. He continues to be optimistic and remains active in his church and in community and civic organizations.

Some days are good, and others are rough, yet he remains a walking miracle in the midst of cancer. He remains a man of faith in the midst of pain because he has discovered his motivational Guide for living.

My friend's zest for life and steadfast faith in the God of deliverance and destiny is a great source of inspiration to me. My friend, like hundreds of thousands of ordinary people who are walking through doorways of destiny in spite of their problems, remains steadfast.

You know them—those facing marital problems and heart-wrenching divorces; those seeking God's face despite the loss of a job; those who weep and worship God in their grief over the death of a loved one; those who wholeheartedly believe that our God is an awesome God even in the midst of pain, problems, and present predicaments; those who boldly declare, "I will fulfill my divine destiny no matter what satan sends to block, stop, or hinder me!"

You may be one of these ordinary people who continues to trust God in the midst of trying circumstances. After all, we are not immune from the bumps and bruises that life brings to all of us at some time or another.

Using Your Positive Potential

Today, as the people of God, we are challenged as never before to arise from the ashes of life. Everyone has a tragedy, a painful memory, a bad experience that has affected us negatively in some way—a friend turns his back on you; someone steals a precious object; an admirer rejects you.

In spite of any heartbreaking, painful experiences that you may have gone through, I challenge you to aspire to rise up and walk through your personal doorway of destiny. Decide to get up and make a difference in the world where you live.

As children of God who are wonderfully and marvelously made in His image, we are full of positive potential.

What does this positive potential mean to you personally? It means you have the potential:

- To succeed and not succumb in the midst of the struggle
- To live, learn, and leave a legacy that is a lifeline to those without hope
- To prepare for a brighter future
- To become a better person

Positive potential, however, is exactly that—potential; but it must be tapped in order to work. Like oil, coal, diamonds, and the vast wealth of riches stored in God's good earth, our potential has to be mined and processed in order to be of value.

The Final Battle Cry

Harriet Tubman, a black woman of destiny, was born in Maryland as a slave. Before she was born, however, Harriet was destined to arise from the vicious chains of bondage and brutal slavery. After escaping to the North, Harriet Tubman risked her life by returning to the South 19 times to free over 350 other slaves.

Why did she risk her life and her freedom for others? Because the Holy Spirit, her personal motivational Guide for living, showed her the way. God used Harriet Tubman—a female Moses and deliverer ordained by God—to open doors of destiny that led those slaves, my ancestors, from captivity to freedom.

Even in the worst of times, you, too, can rise from the ashes of anguish and utter disgust in the worst of times. Why? Because the Creator knows that you have the right stuff within your spirit to overcome any obstacle that stands in your way toward destiny.

Destiny is our battle cry. We must teach every child who is born, "You are a child of destiny. God's hand is on your life."

We must challenge every follower of Jesus Christ to rise from the ashes of anguish to a higher dimension of divine destiny–a new level of Christian growth and maturity.

With an anointed sense of destiny, we will walk together as one body in Christ, the church–made up of all the races of the earth–led by an inter-racial, multi-cultural Savior.

We are a people of destiny called out of the darkness and into the marvelous light to disrupt and demolish the works of satan all over this land.

Rise up, mighty men of valor! Rise up, virtuous women of God! Rise up, chosen children of destiny!

Don't waste time. Get all excited. Get on fire for God. Get motivated by the Holy Ghost now. Take action and occupy until Jesus comes again. That is your destiny.

Jesus' inter-racial makeup makes Him the ultimate argument against racism.

Chapter 12

Shut the Doorways of Deception

"To be born of God means that I have the supernatural power of God to stop sinning."–Oswald Chambers

One day this age of grace will end abruptly. Jesus Christ will crack the eastern skies and return for His own beloved bride–the saints of old, the entire body of Christ, a new race made up of all the races known to man. She will be raptured–caught away in holy ecstasy–and will finally meet Jesus Christ face to face in the air.

God gave the apostle Paul insight into the consummation of this divine romance between Jesus Christ and His church:

Behold, I shew you a mystery; We shall not all sleep, but we shall all be changed, in a moment, in the twinkling of an eye, at the last trump: for the trumpet shall sound, and the dead shall be raised incorruptible, and we shall be changed (1 Corinthians 15:51,52).

The dead in Christ shall rise first: Then we which are alive and remain shall be caught up together with them in the clouds, to meet the Lord in the air: and so shall we ever be with the Lord (1 Thessalonians 4:16,17).

Regarding the signs of the times that point toward this glorious event, Scripture boldly declares:

It is near, even at the doors! (Matthew 24:33).

Matthew began his discourse, however, with a warning:

Take heed that no man deceive you (24:4).

The apostle Paul, in a subsequent letter to the church at Thessalonica, echoed that same admonition regarding the second coming of Christ:

Let no man deceive you by any means (2 Thessalonians 2:3).

We must take their advice and shut the doorway of deception as we draw near to the return of Jesus Christ.

The devil has some devious doors that he desires you to walk through. They are doorways of deception. That old, lying cheat has some dirty, bold-faced lies that he wants you to tell; some bars, dance halls, sleazy theaters, and liquor stores that he wants you to visit. These doorways of deception are designed to steal, kill, and destroy your personal destiny by first destroying your state of mind.

Religious cults, led by people like Jim Jones—who ended up having his followers drink KoolAid laced with cyanide—are doorways of deception. Horoscopes and psychic hotlines are doorways of deception. Thinking they can make it on their own, many Christians trust in themselves and stumble through this doorways of deception.

The horribly lethal "Heaven's Gate" cult is the most modern-day doorway of deception. Satan strategically used this organization to ruin souls, deceiving 21 women and 18 men to commit mass suicide in a $1 million mansion. The victims, ranging in age from 20 to 72, acted on the false hope that they would board a spaceship that would take them to the next level after shedding their physical "vehicles."

God wants us to fulfill our destiny and live life to its fullest. Satan wants to deceive us by telling us that suicide is the way out.

Is there a clear distinction between a divinely opened doorway of destiny and a doorway of deception? Absolutely. Any door that God opens will not lead you to do anything that contradicts His Holy Word and His character.

Our adversary is very cunning, however, and often tries to divert us with the cares of the world. The busy pace of our lives sometimes causes us to miss God's best and our divine destiny.

The Devil's Ways

Someone might ask, "How does the devil stop us from walking through the doorways of destiny?"

One of the first things satan does in January is tell us, "It's okay to start the new year off drinking and dancing up a storm"—instead of bringing in the new year on our knees at a Spirit-filled watch night service and shouting the goodness of God.

In February, when we celebrate African-American History Month, the devil causes so much racial conflict, turmoil, and strife—such as black-on-black crime—that the original purpose of Dr. Carter G. Woodson's African-American History Celebration is put on the national back burner during the shortest month of the year.

In March, we celebrate Women's History Month, and the devil keeps people from walking through the doorways of destiny by making sure sexism is at an all-time high, even in the body of Christ.

Satan surely hates April because Christians celebrate the resurrection of Jesus Christ on Easter. That's when the head of demonic forces tells everybody to focus on the Easter bunny and just forget Jesus Christ Who shed His precious blood for our salvation on Calvary's cross.

In May, June, July, and August, the devil is ready to get busy with some real sinning in the warm weather and sunshine. Satan keeps us from walking through the doorways of destiny in the summer by suggesting it is time to take a vacation from God.

In September, satan says, "Kids, go back to school, but you better not let me catch you praying, or I'll have the school take you to court."

In October, the devil is elated because he thinks it is time to celebrate. All the demons and modern-day witches try to block the saints of God from walking through the doorways of destiny especially on or around Halloween.

In November, the prince of darkness says, "Forget about destiny and Thanksgiving, and let's just pig out!"

When December rolls around, the devil has conditioned hundreds of thousands of church folk to ignore the doorways of destiny. Instead, they celebrate Christmas, forgetting about the Christ child who was born to save the world.

That is how the devil tries to stop us from walking through the doorways of destiny 365 days, 52 weeks, and 12 months of the year.

Sin Lies at the Door

This teaching on walking through the doorways of destiny would be in vain if I failed to warn you that sin also lies at the door. When Cain and Abel offered their sacrifices, God accepted one and not the other. Seeing Cain's anger, God spoke to him:

Why art thou wroth? and why is thy countenance fallen? If thou doest well, shalt thou not be accepted? and if thou doest not well, sin lieth at the door (Genesis 4:6,7).

If we want to truly excel in God, we must deal with the sin in our lives. We may try to ignore it, but it's there. Both individuals and churches need time for self-examination, for:

All have sinned, and come short of the glory of God (Romans 3:23).

God calls the church and the world to confess our sins, repent, and close the doorway of deception. Close the door to drugs. Close the door to alcohol. Close the door to illicit affairs. Close the door to sex before marriage. Close the door to pornography.

Hate also lies at our doors. God calls us to close the door to slanderous lies and deadly gossip. Close the door to jealousy. Close the door to disunity. Close the door to sexism, racism, and anti-semitism. Close the door to the demons that seek to make their home in you, for sin lies at the door. That dirty old devil is knocking at the door of your heart. Don't let him in.

Cain, the firstborn son of Adam and Eve, failed to give God his best offering. When God accepted his brother Abel's offering of the firstling of the flock, and rejected his own offering of the fruit of the land, Cain grew angry. The devil stroked his smoldering emotions. Satan oppressed him through his mind. Cain eventually killed Abel, committing the first murder in human history.

When God confronted Cain before He sent him east of Eden, the murderer asked:

Am I my brother's keeper? (Genesis 4:9).

Cain hadn't grasped the truth, but the answer is yes, I am my brother's keeper. Our job is to help people fulfill their potential for greatness—their personal and corporate destiny—and not crush someone's hopes, dreams, and aspirations for the future.

God is calling us to a divine destiny. Are we attaining a place in God where we can honestly say:

I had rather be a doorkeeper in the house of my God, than to dwell in the tents of wickedness (Psalm 84:10).

God calls us to close the doors of our spirit, mind, and body to all the negative forces of evil that seek to control us. We must open these same doors only to those relationships that are divinely orchestrated and ordained by the Master of our destiny, Jesus Christ.

Don't Stop Now

In the midst of seasons that seem strangely out of line at times, I encourage you to walk through your doorway of destiny. You will pass through many developmental stages in your Christian journey. Make sure you don't get stuck on any one plateau. Keep pressing on to attain all God has for you.

You may see terrorism such as the bomb that killed an innocent woman at the 1996 Olympics in Atlanta, Georgia. You may read about discrimination such as the Texaco corporate executives calling African-American employees black jelly beans. Network news may shock you with the aftermath of deadly explosions such the fatal blast on TWA flight 800 off the coast of Long Island that took the lives of 230 people headed for Paris.

Despite tragedy and injustice in this life, God has promised to open many doors for His people. Scripture affirms that God has supplied these entrances for those who belong to Him:

1. The door of hope (Hosea 2:15).
2. The door of faith (Acts 14:27).
3. The door of utterance (Colossians 4:3).

4. The door of opportunity (Revelation 3:8).
5. The door of fellowship (Revelation 3:20).
6. The door in heaven (Revelation 4:1).

In fact, there are twelve gates in the heavenly city: three in the east, three in the west, three in the north, and three in the south. These twelve gates lead to the Door of the sheep, Jesus Christ, who is the only way (John 10:7-9). Twelve celestial doorways of destiny point to the eternal Door of the sheep.

Knowing the focal point of our destiny, we can lift our bowed down heads and our troubled hearts to our Eternal Shepherd. He wants to recharge, renew, and restore us. With the help of Jesus Christ, we can live an abundant life no matter what's going on in our lives.

We can also turn our attention to the tortured souls of men, women, boys, and girls of every single race, nationality, and creed on the face of the earth. Let us extend a hand to those who are despised, disfranchised, and despondent.

The enemy has lied to them about Who God is and who they can become in Jesus Christ. Through the preaching of the gospel, we can help them shut the doorways of deception. We can also encourage them to open the doors of their lives to Jesus Christ.

Lift up your heads, O ye gates; and be ye lift up, ye everlasting doors; and the King of glory shall come in. Who is this King of glory? The Lord strong and mighty, the Lord mighty in battle . . . The Lord of hosts, he is the King of glory (Psalm 24:7,8,10).

If we allow Jesus Christ to rule in our lives, to reveal His destiny for us, and to accomplish it by the power of His Spirit, we will experience lives that soar far above the commonplace. We can extend this same hope to those who are floundering without a sense of destiny.

The Right Door

People who lack God-given purpose unknowingly open themselves to the devil's schemes. The enemy presents many temptations to entice them to walk through the door of sin. We can share insights from Scripture and personal experience to help them shut these doorways of deception.

Think about doors as points of access for new experiences. Let's look at it from both a natural and spiritual perspective.

I walk through many physical doorways daily. When I wake up, I praise the Lord, greet my wife, wipe the sleep from my eyes, get out of bed, and walk through the bedroom door. I open the door to the baby's room and check on Yolanda. Then I proceed to the bathroom door.

After I wash and dress, I open the front door, walk downstairs, and open the porch door. From there I open the car door, drive to the office, and walk through large glass doors.

When Brenda and I go to the supermarket, we walk to the main entrance, and the doors open automatically. When we go to church and I unlock the doors, we walk into the vestibule and open the doors to the sanctuary.

All these doors are natural doorways. Different doors give us access to different things, depending upon what we're looking for. If I need toothpaste, I walk through the bathroom door and look in the cabinet. I don't open the refrigerator or garbage can to look for my toothpaste, mouthwash, or deodorant.

Luke 11:9,10 states:

And I say unto you, Ask, and it shall be given you; seek, and ye shall find; knock, and it shall be opened unto you. For every one that asketh receiveth; and he that seeketh findeth; and to him that knocketh it shall be opened.

Be careful whose door you're knocking on because someone just might answer. Make sure you're asking, seeking, and knocking about positive things that will glorify God.

When I need more power and guidance to make it through the day, I knock on the heart of my Father God through prayer, praise, and worship. This door gives me access to His divine presence and glory.

This world offers us many different doorways. Each one gives us access to different experiences. Our culture tempts us to walk through many dangerous doors—drug abuse, pornography, and illicit sex—that prove harmful to our spiritual growth. Once we've crossed the threshold of these experiences, it becomes very easy to return there. We need discerning hearts to walk through the right door.

When God Closes a Door

Sometimes we may not even be aware that a seemingly good thing may be detrimental to us. Our wise, loving Father often prevents us from entering these realms. During these times we must trust God's judgment and:

Lean not unto thine own understanding (Proverbs 3:5).

I am glad I serve a God Who knows when to open and close doors in our lives. Open doors are a sign of opportunity and upcoming persecution for the sake of the gospel. Closed doors are a sign to seek the face of God more earnestly in the times of preparation.

Alexander Graham Bell once stated:

When one door closes, another opens; but we often look so long and so regretfully upon the closed door that we do not see the one that has opened for us.

Instead of regretting the doors that God closes in our lives, we should praise Him for it—for He knows what is best—and begin to focus on closing the devil's doorways of deception. If we shut out the devil, God can begin to open doors in our lives. For he is the God that:

> Commanded the clouds from above, and opened the doors of heaven (Psalm 78:23).

Sometimes it may seem that we'll never pass through our doorway of destiny. Don't let the devil discourage you or steal your hope in God's promises. When the anointing of the Holy Spirit comes upon you and the timing is right, God will do a mighty work.

Rise Up and Walk

The apostle Luke, a physician who authored the Acts of the Apostles, wrote about a lame man who lay before a tremendous doorway of destiny—the gate known as Beautiful, the entrance to the temple. This huge doorway of destiny, an entrance of thanksgiving, was an awesome architectural structure of great significance to the thousands of Jewish worshippers who walked through it on a daily basis.

This lame man had been carried to this doorway every single day of his life, ever since his mother gave birth to him. It is also believed that Jesus Christ Himself, the Master of Destiny, walked through this very gate. This lame man, who lay there every day, was not healed when Jesus passed him.

I mention this to show how foolish it is to look down on someone who has not received the physical manifestation of divine healing. God may not show up when you want Him to, but He is always right on time. It pays to wait on the Lord, for He will renew our strength.

Now Peter and John went up together into the temple at the hour of prayer, being the ninth hour. And a certain man lame from his mother's womb was carried, whom they laid daily at the gate of the temple which is called Beautiful, to ask alms of them that entered into the temple; Who seeing Peter and John about to go into the temple asked an alms.

And Peter, fastening his eyes upon him with John, said, Look on us. And he gave heed unto them, expecting to receive something of them.

Then Peter said, Silver and gold have I none; but such as I have give I thee: In the name of Jesus Christ of Nazareth rise up and walk.

And he took him by the right hand, and lifted him up: and immediately his feet and ancle bones received strength. And he leaping up stood, and walked, and entered with them into the temple, walking, and leaping, and praising God. And all the people saw him walking and praising God: And they knew that it was he which sat for alms at the Beautiful gate of the temple: and they were filled with wonder and amazement at that which had happened unto him.

And as the lame man which was healed held Peter and John, all the people ran together unto them in the porch that is called Solomon's, greatly wondering (Acts 3:1-11).

Peter and John saw the lame man begging as they entered the temple grounds to worship. At the ninth hour, or 3:00 p.m., Peter and John focused their eyes on the lame man, and said, "Look on us!" These men had the anointing of the Holy Spirit upon them. This lame man wanted money, but Peter and John gave him something that he never expected—the ability to walk through his own doorway of destiny and worship God in the temple.

Lean on God's Ability

If you are in a wheelchair or have no legs, you can rise up and walk in your spirit. If you are on crutches, your body may hobble around but that doesn't have to limit your spirit and soul. One day, whether it is here on earth or in heaven, God will renew your strength.

Don't be discouraged about your disability. Lean on the ability and power of God. You can also rise above the ashes of despair and hopelessness and be greatly used by God. God is no respecter of persons.

Thank God for those who get out of wheelchairs and throw away crutches at crusades, for God is able to deliver. I know that beyond a shadow of a doubt. God is a healer. There is no debate about it.

Yet I also thank God for righteous men and women who worship despite their limitations. They may still be in wheelchairs or use crutches. They may not have hands or the ability to see, hear, or walk.

These unsung heroes, who haven't received the manifestation of their healing, still sing, rise up, and walk through their own personal doorways of destiny. They leap and rejoice deeply within their own sanctified souls day by day. They are living epistles of Jesus Christ Who still believe in the Healer whether or not they have received the physical manifestation of healing.

Lift Someone Up

Peter boldly declared to the lame man, "Silver and gold have I none; but such as I have give I thee: In the name of Jesus Christ of Nazareth rise up and walk" (vs. 6).

Notice what Peter did. After he spoke the word in Jesus' name, he helped the lame man. Verse 7 says, "And he took him by the right hand, and lifted him up: and immediately his feet and ancle bones received strength."

Why do so many people fail to gain the victory over their problems? Once we boldly speak the word in Jesus' name, we don't follow through. We forget to reach out and lift our brothers and sisters out of the pit of despair.

Peter said, "Rise up and walk." With a little help from Peter, the lame man leaped up, stood on his feet for the first time in his life, and walked through the gate called Beautiful. Passing through that doorway of destiny, he leaped for joy. Even though Jesus hadn't healed him during His earthly ministry, the power of His Spirit raised him up at this time.

It may have seemed like the Lord had passed him by, but Jesus had not forgotten him, and the Lord has not forgotten you. Whether your healing manifests in this lifetime, or when you pass through the pearly gates and you see Jesus face to face, remember that Jesus loves you, and He will never leave you or forsake you.

You Can Do It!

Determine to rise up from your personal seat of despair and self-pity and walk through your doorway of destiny. Nobody can stop you from reaching your full potential except you. It is not controlled by the standards of man. No matter what your condition, you can rise up and walk and begin to make a difference in someone's life.

Catch the vision of victory and never give up. Begin to do all you can right now, for the angel's lips are at the trumpet. The Master is waiting for the last prophecy to be fulfilled, the last choir to sing, the last preacher to preach, the last altar call to be made, and the last soul to be saved.

Listen to the words of James, the earthly brother of our Savior Jesus Christ.

Be ye also patient; stablish your hearts: for the coming of the Lord draweth nigh. Grudge not one against another, brethren, lest ye be condemned; behold, the judge standeth before the door (James 5:8,9).

The doorways of destiny, the doors of grace and divinely appointed opportunity, will not always be open. Take advantage of it now because this dispensation of grace is not forever. Judgment day is coming quickly, and this age of grace will end.

While we have opportunity, let us rise up and walk through the portals of God-ordained purpose. We can be all that God intends for us to be while the doorways of destiny remain open.

About the Author

Rev. Arthur L. Mackey, Jr., Founder and President of Visions of Victory Ministries, travels nationally and internationally, preaching the Gospel of Jesus Christ.

He is a graduate of Virginia Union University in Richmond, Virginia where he majored in Religion and Philosophy.

Rev. Mackey, Jr. serves as Assistant Pastor of the Mt. Sinai Baptist Church in Roosevelt, New York, and is called of God to motivational ministry.

He and his lovely wife, Brenda Jackson Mackey, have one daughter, Yolanda.

Scripture References

And when they were come, and had gathered the church together, they rehearsed all that God had done with them, and how he had opened the door of faith unto the Gentiles (Acts 14:27).

For a great door and effectual is opened unto me, and there are many adversaries (1 Corinthians 16:9).

Furthermore, when I came to Troas to preach Christ's gospel, and a door was opened unto me of the Lord (2 Corinthians 2:12).

Continue in prayer, and watch in the same with thanksgiving; withal praying also for us, that God would open unto us a door of utterance, to speak the mystery of Christ, for which I am also in bonds (Colossians 4:2,3).

Grudge not one against another, brethren, lest ye be condemned: behold, the judge standeth before the door (James 5:9).

I know thy works: behold, I have set before thee an open door, and no man can shut it: for thou hast a little strength, and hast kept my word, and hast not denied my name.... Behold, I stand at the door, and knock: if any man hear my voice, and open the door, I will come in to him, and will sup with him, and he with me.... After this I looked, and, behold, a door was open in heaven: and the first voice which I heard was as it were of a trumpet talking with me; which said, Come up hither, and I will show thee things which must be hereafter (Revelation 3:8,20, 4:1).

God keeps on opening doors!

Selected Bibliography

Bonhoeffer, Dietrich. *The Cost of Discipleship*. New York: Collier Books, McMillan Publishing Company, 1963.

Carmen, Licciardello. *Raising the Standard: Reclaiming Our World for God*. Nashville: Sparrow Press, 1994.

Chambers, Oswald. *My Utmost for His Highest*. Uhrichsville, Ohio: Barbour and Company, Inc., 1963.

King Jr., Dr. Martin Luther. *The Measure of a Man*. Philadelphia: Fortress Press, 1988.

Notes

1. C. D. Martin, *His Eye Is On The Sparrow: The New National Baptist Hymnal* (Nashville, TN: 1990), p. 204.

2. Francis A. Schaeffer, *The Church at the End of the 20th Century: Including the Church Before the Watching World* (Wheaton, IL: Crossway Books, 1985), p. 5.

3. *American Psychiatric Glossary* (Washington, DC: American Psychiatric Press, Inc., 1988), p. 2.

4. Carman Licciardello, *Raising the Standard: Reclaiming Our World For God* (Nashville: Sparrow Press, 1994), pp. 194, 195.

5. Martin Luther King, Jr., *The Measure of a Man* (Philadelphia, PA: Fortress Press, 1988), p. 56.

6. Oswald Chambers, *My Utmost For His Highest* (Uhrichsville, OH: Barbour and Company, Inc., 1963), p. 245.

7. Ibid., p. 307.

OTHER BOOKS FROM
Pneuma Life Publishing

The Biblical Principles of Success
Arthur L. Mackey, Jr.

There are only three types of people in the world: People who make things happen, People who watch things happen, and People who do not know what in the world is happening. *The Biblical Principles of Success* will help you become one who makes things happen. Success is not a matter of "doing it my way." It is turning from a personal, selfish philosophy to God's outreaching, sharing way of life. This powerful book teaches you how to tap into success principles that are guaranteed! Rev. Mackey is also the author of *Inner Healing for Men* and *Inner Healing for Women*.

The Minister's Topical Bible
by Derwin Stewart

The Minister's Topical Bible covers every aspect of the ministry providing quick and easy access to Scriptures in a variety of ministry related topics. This handy reference tool can be effectively used in leadership training, counseling, teaching, sermon preparation, and personal study.

The Believer's Topical Bible
by Derwin Stewart

The Believer's Topical Bible covers every aspect of a Christian's relationship with God and man, providing biblical answers and solutions for many challenges. It is a quick, convenient, and thorough reference Bible that has been designed for use in personal devotions and group Bible studies. with over 3,800 verses systematically organized under 240 topics, it is the largest devotional-topical Bible available in the New International Version and the King James Version.

The Harvest
by T. D. Jakes

God's heart beats for lost and dying humanity. The Church, however, has a tremendous shortage of sold-out, unselfish Christians committed to the salvation and discipleship of the lost. This disillusioned generation hungers for lasting reality. Are we ready to offer them eternal hope in Jesus Christ? without a passion for holiness, sanctification, and evangelism, we will miss the greatest harvest of the ages. God has ordained the salvation of one final crop of souls and given us the privilege of putting in the sickle. Allow God to set you ablaze. Seize the opportunity of a lifetime and become an end-time laborer in the Church's finest hour! *Workbook also available*

Help Me! I've Fallen
by T. D. Jakes

"Help! I've fallen, and I can't get up." This cry, made popular by a familiar television commercial, points out the problem faced by many Christians today. Have you ever stumbled and fallen with no hope of getting up? Have you been wounded and hurt by others? Are you so far down you think you'll never stand again? Don't despair. All Christians fall from time to time. Life knocks us off balance, making it hard – if not impossible – to get back on our feet. The cause of the fall is not as important as what we do while we're down. T. D. Jakes explains how – and Whom – to ask for help. In a struggle to regain your balance, this book is going to be your manual to recovery! Don't panic. This is just a test!

Becoming A Leader
by Myles Munroe

Many consider leadership to be no more than staying ahead of the pack, but that is a far cry from what leadership is. Leadership is deploying others to become as good as or better than you are. within each of us lies the potential to be an effective leader. *Becoming A Leader* uncovers the secrets of dynamic leadership that will show you how to be a leader in your family, school, community, church and job. No matter where you are or what you do in life this book can help you to inevitably become a leader. Remember: it is never too late to become a leader. As in every tree there is a forest, so in every follower there is a leader. *Workbook also available*

The God Factor
by James Giles

Is something missing in your life? Do you find yourself at the mercy of your circumstances? Is your self-esteem at an all-time low? Are your dreams only a faded memory? You could be missing the one element that could make the difference between success and failure, poverty and prosperity, and creativity and apathy. Knowing God supplies the creative genius you need to reach your potential and realize your dream. You'll be challenged as James Giles shows you how to tap into your God-given genius, take steps toward reaching your goal, pray big and get answers, eat right and stay healthy, prosper economically and personally, and leave a lasting legacy for your children.

The Flaming Sword
by Tai Ikomi
Scripture memorization and meditation bring tremendous spiritual power, however many Christians find it to be an uphill task. Committing Scriptures to memory will transform the mediocre Christian to a spiritual giant. This book will help you to become addicted to the powerful practice of Scripture memorization and help you obtain the victory that you desire in every area of your life. *Flaming Sword* is your pathway to spiritual growth and a more intimate relationship with God.

Come, Let Us Pray!
by J. Emmette Weir
Like an ocean, prayer is so vast that we will never plumb its depths. Are you content to walk along the shore, or are you ready to launch out into the deep? No matter what your stage of spiritual development, you can learn to pray with greater intimacy, gratitude, and power. Discover the secrets of personal prayer in *Come, Let Us Pray!*

Available at your local bookstore